ANCIENT & MEDIAEVAL SCULPTURED STONES OF ISLAY

ANCIENT & MEDIAEVAL SCULPTURED STONES OF ISLAY

W. D. LAMONT

JOHN SMITH & SON (GLASGOW) LTD
GLASGOW

JOHN SMITH & SON (GLASGOW) LTD
57 St. Vincent Street
Glasgow G2 5TB

First Published (Oliver & Boyd) 1968
Paperback Edition (John Smith & Son) 1972

SBN 05 001651 2

SBN 900673 - 06 - 0

Printed in Great Britain by
Mitchell & Moreland Ltd., Glasgow

PREFACE

Rather more than seventy years ago R. C. Graham's *Carved Stones of Islay* recorded the ancient and mediaeval stones then known in the island, and only a few additional ones have since come to light. The majority of his excellent plates are from photographs either of the original monuments or of carefully made casts; and the book is of outstanding value, for nothing comparable in quantity or quality could be produced today, many of the items having in the interval disappeared or greatly deteriorated.

Unfortunately the volume is very scarce; and as it is unlikely to be reprinted within the foreseeable future, a booklet covering at least a selection of the material may be welcome to residents and visitors alike. The following pages are therefore based on Graham's work.

The method of treatment, however, is somewhat different. Graham's essential purpose was to catalogue, describe and illustrate, and he resisted the temptation to propound general theories. But during the past half century comparative study has thrown some light on the relation of the Islay stones to those in other parts of the British Isles; and as people interested in the stones will also be interested in their historical context, I have attempted to place the different types in some sort of order and to indicate noteworthy features in particular cases.

It must be confessed that some of the views here adopted are stated with an assurance which ignores serious cleavage in expert opinion, but it is hoped that, for those wishing to pursue the subject, a corrective to this over-simplification will be found in the bibliography on page 60.

Those familiar with the Islay stones may be disappointed to find no reference to some of their favourites; but to leave space for comparative illustration selection has been inevitable. It is hoped, however, that the *types* covered will serve as a general guide with respect to examples not specifically mentioned.

At this point a general warning may be given. Usually,

though not invariably, I refer to the stones as they were located when Graham wrote. Many have been moved since then; but it seems desirable to preserve the reference to the original sites, so far as known. If this will not secure the re-discovery of them all, it will at least make clear the extent of the loss.

In acknowledging our indebtedness to Graham we do not forget those who encouraged and assisted him in the enterprise, most continuously, perhaps, the Ramsays of Kildalton. No one investigating the history and antiquities of the island can fail to be impressed by the care which, over three generations, they have devoted to the collection and preservation of its historical records and the material antiquities falling under their charge.

More recently a noteworthy contribution to our knowledge of our heritage has been made by the Islay Archaeological Survey Group. Its *Gazetteer*, with Supplements, is now a standard work of reference.

The short bibliography will indicate the type of published material I have found most useful; and for consulting such works and the relevant periodicals I have had the advantage of ranging freely in Glasgow University Library. The main disadvantage of such liberty is that the rich provision offered makes one painfully aware of how little one knows and how much there is to learn.

It also emphasises the patchy results of 'teach yourself'. Fortunately I have not been wholly dependent on this method and was able to submit earlier drafts of the booklet to more qualified students in the field. It gives me great pleasure to acknowledge the kindness of Dr J. X. W. P. Corcoran of Glasgow University and Colonel A. R. Cross, of Dr Kenneth Steer of the Royal Commission on the Ancient and Historical Monuments of Scotland and Mr R. B. K. Stevenson, Keeper of the National Museum of Antiquities, for helping me to a better understanding of the material with which I was coping, and consequently to seeing the Islay stones in sharper focus. I hope they may recognise some reflection of themselves, however distorted, in the relevant sections of this final product.

The cost of producing a work of this kind is considerable, and I greatly appreciate the generous assistance granted by the Carnegie Trust for the Universities of Scotland.

Illustrations. Most of the illustrations of the Islay stones are copied from Graham's *Carved Stones of Islay*.

I am also indebted:

To J. Romilly Allen's *Early Christian Monuments of Scotland* for the Aberlemno stone shewn on IV *b*.

To C. H. Ashdown's *British and Foreign Arms and Armour* for XXIV *c*.

To the publishers of W. G. Collingwood's *Northumbrian Crosses of the Pre-Norman Age* for permission to reproduce the cross-slab X *a* and the examples of vine-scroll on XII.

To Mr T. M. Crawford, Headmaster of Bowmore School, for the opportunity to photograph cross-slabs V *b* and IX *b* and the Laggan cross-shaft XXXI *a*.

To E. L. Cutts' *Manual of Sepulchral Slabs and Crosses* for the cross-slabs X *b*, *c* and *d*, and XVIII *a*.

To J. Drummond's *Sculptured Monuments of Iona and the West Highlands* for the Iona cross-slabs XIII *a* and *b*, XV *c* and XVIII *b*, the warrior effigy XXIV *b* and the MacIan stone XXV *c*.

To Mr R. Hodkinson, Bowmore, for the opportunity to photograph the Laggan cross-slab IX *d*.

To the Islay Archaeological Survey Group for the chapel site II *a*.

To P. M. C. Kermode's *Manx Crosses* for the cross-head XXVIII *b*.

To the Royal Irish Academy and Dr Henry for permission to reproduce the monastic site I *a*.

To the Society of Antiquaries of Scotland for permission to reproduce the illustrations XI *a* and *b*.

To the National Museum of Antiquities of Scotland for permission to photograph the cross-slabs III *b*, V *d* and IX *a*, and the two cross-heads XXIX *c* nd XXX *a*.

To J. Stuart's *Sculptured Stones of Scotland* for the cross and shaft on XXVII.

To Captain T. P. White's *Archaeological Sketches in Scotland, Kintyre* (1873), and *Knapdale* (1875), for the Knapdale cross-slabs XIII *c* and *d*, and XXII *b* and *c*; the Kintyre cross-shaft XIX *b*; and the warrior effigy XXIV *a*.

PREFACE TO THE SECOND EDITION

The first edition, published in 1968, was sold out by October 1969, and though the possibilities of a reprint were then discussed, the production difficulties have only now been surmounted by the adoption of a photo-litho reissue in paperback.

This has precluded any revision of the original text, and the following pages of addenda and corrigenda are rather an inferior substitute. It is hoped, however, that they will be of value to readers interested in points of detail.

Among the many contributions of Mrs Iain Ramsay, I referred on p. 8 to her discovery of the three stones at the chapel in Gleann na Gaoithe. It is interesting to learn that this was a local rediscovery, Mr Stewart Cruden, Inspector of Ancient Monuments, having recorded them some years previously during a visit to the island.

I am further in her debt for clearing up a minor mystery. Of the two cross-heads, Islay Nos. 108 and 109, now in the National Museum of Antiquities, nothing was known apart from the fact that they had been presented by Captain Ramsay. Mrs Ramsay has very kindly sent me extracts from the note-books of his mother, Mrs Lucy Ramsay, which record that round about 1881 No. 108 was found during the dismantling of a wall in the steading of Kintour farm, and that No. 109 was at Tighcarmagan, near Port Ellen.

The reproduction of Graham's churchyard plans on p. 55 has borne unexpected fruit. The cross-head fragment and section of shaft, Kilarow 28 (XXIX, *b*) had long been given up as lost when Mr and Mrs Beswick, during a systematic survey of the grounds, took soundings at the appropriate spot and uncovered them both. An even more exciting achievement—this time without benefit of Graham—was their discovery in the churchyard at Kilchoman of a warrior slab which is quite unique in Islay. The particulars are given in Addenda and Corrigenda, note to p. 38.

ADDENDA AND CORRIGENDA

p. 8. Gleann na Gaoithe 73a (III, *a*): There are also some large stones of this type in Argyll—one at St Ninian's Chapel, Sanda Island, near the Mull of Kintyre, and several of an impressive size on Eilean Fhinain in Loch Shiel.

p. 13. Port Ellen Area 77 (V, *d*): There is a similar ringed-cross stone at Cladh a' Bhile near Ellery in Knapdale.

pp. 25ff. Islay Long-cross and Foliage slabs 8, 29, 89 and 99 (XIV): The notes on these stones require some clarification and correction.

Firstly, the suggestion that the 'long-cross' slab is the primary form of recumbent decorated stone refers only to the stones of Islay. There are other 'long-cross' slabs in the West Highlands, e.g. at Kilmartin in Knapdale and even in Iona itself, on the relative dating of which we have no view to offer.

Secondly, the reference strictly speaking is only to three of the Islay slabs, namely 8, 29 and 99, the cross-head of 89 (XIV, *c*) having a different form. But the three in question are so distinctive that their period and provenance can be determined with reasonable confidence. They are quite clearly products of a particular Iona school (XIII, *a* and *b*) and apparently few in number. The only examples known to the present writer are *four* in Iona, *three* in Islay (Finlaggan 10 was included in error), and *one* at Keills in Morvern.

Thirdly, the existence of the Morvern example, with which the writer has only recently become acquainted, strengthens the hypothesis that the type belongs to the reign of John 1st Lord of the Isles. The neighbouring castle of Ardtornish was one of his principal administrative centres, and it was there that he died in 1380.

p. 30, lines 3 and 4: There are in fact only *four* known 'long-cross' slabs in Islay. Finlaggan 10 was accepted on Graham's authority; but though the designs on this stone are now almost completely obliterated, the faint traces of a galley at the top show that it belongs to a different and later class.

p. 37, line 14: for 'riggings' read 'rigging'.

p. 38. Warrior Effigies: A slab discovered in 1969 by Mr and Mrs Beswick in Kilchoman churchyard is not only the sole 'warrior' known to exist in the Rhinns but is also unique in Islay. It is a small stone with double-roll moulding, 41 in. long by 15 in. at the head and narrowing to 12½ in. at the foot. The effigy, instead of occupying the whole slab in characteristic Islay fashion, is only 18 in. long, with the left hand at the scabbard and the right holding an upright spear. The whole design suggests that it was made in Knapdale; and the fact that it had to be transported to Islay might account for its small size. It should be added to the Index, p. 53, as 'Kilchoman 51a'.

p. 41. '(5) Ecclesiastics', first sentence: see preceding note to p. 38.

p. 42, middle of page: 'two Islay cross-heads'. These have now been identified. See below, notes to pp. 43 and 44.

p. 43. Islay 108 (XXIX, *c*): Apparently unknown to Graham, the stone was found about 1881 at Kintour farmhouse. Probably came originally from the environs of Kildalton Church.

p. 44. Islay 109 (XXX, *a* and *b*): This is the 'cross' at Tigh-carmagan mentioned by Mrs Lucy Ramsay (see p. 22 of the text). Since the house is a modern one which has simply assumed an old local name and has no religious associations, it is possible that the cross-head was brought there from the vicinity of Kilnaughton Church. This, however, is no more than a guess.

p. 47. Kilarow 31 (XXXI, *c*): The Rev J. G. MacNeill who spent much of his early life in Islay says (*New Guide to Islay* (1900), p. 67) that it was Mr Hugh Morrison who moved the Judge's Cross from *Clachan an Tachair* (*sic* for *Clach an t-Ach' Bhreitheimh*, Stone of the Judge's Field) and erected it on *Cnoc na Croiche* at Kilarow. This strengthens the suggestion that the name on the shaft is 'Patrick'. He may well have been the Patrick McBriuin who witnessed the charter of Donald 2nd Lord of the Isles granting extensive lands in the Oa and Machrie area to Brian Vicar MacKay, a cadet of the MacKays of the Rhinns of Islay.

p. 48. Kilchoman 39 (XXXV): A line of the inscription has been omitted. The correct reading is:

HEC EST C
RUX . . . .
. . E. . . . .
. TRIC . . . .
DI . . PRO A
NIMA SUI PAT
RIS ET MATR
IS ET UXORI
S SUE AC OMN
IUM FIDELIUM
D E F U N C T O R
UM ET DICTI.
. . . . . T. . . . . . .
. . . .

THIS IS THE CROSS OF . . . . . ? . . . [made] . . . FOR THE SOUL OF HIS FATHER AND HIS MOTHER AND HIS WIFE AND (THE SOULS) OF ALL FAITHFUL DEPARTED AND THE SAID . . . . ? . . . .

p. 52. Finlaggan 10: For 'Slab: long-cross, foliage, sword' read 'Slab: design virtually obliterated, but faint trace of galley at top'.

p. 54. Islay 108: Add 'found at Kintour farm'.

p. 54. Islay 109: Add 'from Tighcarmagan, Port Ellen Area'.

CONTENTS

PLATES

The numbers assigned to Islay stones refer to Graham's Index, see pp. 52-54.

I. ANCIENT IRISH ORATORIES:

a. Church Island, Co Kerry (from F. Henry)
b. Oratory at Kells, probably completed A.D. 814.

II. ANCIENT CHAPELS IN ISLAY:

a. Kilsleven (from IASG). Note western doorway and circular enclosure.
b. Cil Eileagain (near Craigens)
c. Tokamol, in The Oa
d. Gleann na Gaoithe (from IASG)

III. EARLY ISLAY CROSS-SLABS (Style A.D. 500-750):

a. Gleann na Gaoithe N.o 73a, a roughly shaped cross.
b. Kildalton No. 79a, a slab with incised outline cross, found interred under Kildalton High Cross.
c. Kildalton No. 88.
d. Kilchoman No. 54, a combination of three crosses.

IV. IRISH AND PICTISH MONUMENTS:

a. Ahenny South Cross
b. Aberlemno No. 2 (from J. Romilly Allen)
c. Ahenny North Cross

V. ISLAY RING-CROSS SLABS (dating controversial):

a. Gleann na Gaoithe No. 73b
b. Eilean Orsay No. 73d
c. Kilchoman No. 55, a shafted ring-cross in relief.
d. Port Ellen Area No. 77, originally at Kilbride.

XIV. 'LONG-CROSS' SLABS, ISLAY:

a. Finlaggan No. 8
b. Kilarow No. 29
c. Kildalton No. 89
d. Kildalton No. 99

XV. ELIPTICAL OR HEART SHAPED FOLIAGE:

a. Finlaggan No. 7
b. Keills No. 1, slab with later inscription
c. 'Angus MacDonald' slab, Iona (from J. Drummond)
d. Kilnaughton No. 76

XVI. 'SINGLE-STEM SERPENTINE' FOLIAGE:

a. Kilarow No. 23, with intricate geometrical cross-head, sword, 'heart shaped' foliage on dexter side, and 'ring' form of 'single-stem serpentine' on sinister side.
b. Nereabolls No. 72, with 'ring serpentine' on sinister and 'open serpentine' on dexter side.
c. Kilchoman No. 41, with 'open serpentine'.
d. Nereabolls No. 73, with degenerate 'open serpentine' in sinister panel.

XVII. LATER SLABS AND APPROPRIATED STONES:

a. Kilarow No. 20 and b. Kilarow No. 30, slabs with degenerate foliage, well carved animals, and late 15th-16th century claymores.
c. Kilchoman No. 40, 15th century slab appropriated by Campbells in 17th century.
d. Kilarow No. 16, considerably altered in 17th century by Frasers.

XVIII. 'VINE AND BRANCHES' DESIGN:

a. 14th century slab at Hexham (from E. L. Cutts)
b. Slab in Iona (from J. Drummond)
c. Nereabolls No. 70

XIX. DECORATIVE MOTIVES, ISLAY AND KINTYRE:

a. Nereabolls No. 71
b. Shaft of cross at Campbeltown with animal group at bottom similar to that at dexter side of sword-hilt in a.

XXVII. MEDIAEVAL CROSSES, HEADS WITH GEOMETRICAL PATTERNS:

a. Keills No. 2, shaft only, but head presumably as on b (from J. Stuart)

XXVIII. MEDIAEVAL CROSSES, HEADS WITH GEOMETRICAL PATTERNS:

a. Kildalton No. 80
b. Manx cross-head (from Kermode)

XXIX. MEDIAEVAL CROSSES, HEADS WITH GEOMETRICAL PATTERNS:

a. Kildalton No. 80, East and West faces.
b. Kilarow No. 28 (reconstruction)
c. Islay No. 108, cross-head in Nat. Mus. of Antiq., Edinburgh.

XXX. DISC-HEADED CROSSES:

a. & b. Islay No. 109, part of cross-head now in Nat. Mus. of Antiq., Edinburgh.
c. Texa Nos. 103 and 104, figures from a disc-headed cross now in Nat. Mus. of Antiq., Edinburgh.
d. Kilchoman No. 53, head and part of shaft.

XXXI. DISC-HEADED CROSSES:

a. Laggan No. 32a, cross-shaft with lower part of Crucifixion on obverse and late 15th-16th century scroll on reverse.
b. Texa No. 105, shaft of cross commemorating 'Reginald son of John of Islay'.
c. Kilarow No. 31

XXXII. DISC-HEADED CROSSES:

a. Kilchoman No. 52, cross-head with figures by the cross and single-stem foliage on reverse.
b. Kilchoman No. 47, cross-shaft with lower part of Crucifixion and ecclesiastic on obverse, with fine 'open serpentine' on reverse.

XXXIII. DISC-HEADED CROSSES:

Nereabolls Nos. 62 and 63, head and part of shaft of (?MacKay) cross.

These plates are placed at the end of the volume.

I

ANCIENT CROSSES: SLABS AND FREE-STANDING

Introductory

The Ancient Celtic Church

Although the disciples of St Ninian were evangelising Scotland from Whithorn in the late 4th century, for the effective introduction of Christianity to Islay we are indebted to missionaries from Ireland, probably in the late 5th or early 6th century.

As it reached Argyll and the Hebrides, the organisation of the Celtic church was wholly monastic. This was unusual if not unique in western Europe, and it affected both the internal government of the church and its relations with the people of the land.

With respect to church government, the usual system resembled that of modern Catholicism or the Church of England. Primarily, the organised church meant the system of territorial 'dioceses' or 'sees', each under its bishop in whom were combined both sacerdotal and administrative authority. On the one hand, it was through the consecrated episcopate alone that apostolic authority and priestly office could be transmitted; and, on the other hand, the bishop was the administrative head of his diocese which was subdivided into parishes under the care of subordinate clergy. There were, of course, monastic communities living under their appropriate rules and to some degree independent of the territorial system; but they were not an essential constituent, so to speak, of the church visible.

In the ancient Celtic west, however, the monastic orders were themselves the church visible, for there was no diocesan system. One of the characteristics of this peculiar situation was that sacerdotal and administrative power were quite distinct. The monastic communities scattered over the country were very much alike in general character but distinguished by their allegiance to different 'mother churches'. Broadly speaking, a monastery acknowledged as its mother church the community to which its founder had belonged, and some of the greater monasteries such as Clonard, Clonmacnoise and Monasterboice (all in Ireland) became the headquarters of powerful ecclesiastical confederations. To envisage the ancient Celtic system of church government, then, we have to think, not of a country divided territorially into 'sees', but of confederations of religious houses—often intermingled territorially—the administrative head of each confederation being the abbot of its 'mother church'.

So far as his rank in holy orders was concerned, this abbot might be a mere priest or presbyter, as was the case with St Columba and most of his successors in Iona. For this reason some have supposed that the Columban church was 'presbyterian', not 'episcopal'; but this is a misunderstanding. Presbyterianism and episcopacy are both essentially territorial systems of administration, differing in their conceptions of holy orders and apostolic authority. But though the Columban church was not a territorial system in the same sense, the unique status of the bishop was fully accepted. Thus, in the celebration of the Mass and in other liturgical offices St Columba always yielded precedence to any resident or visiting bishop, but this precedence was on purely sacerdotal grounds. Administrative authority was a function of the monastic brotherhood. A prior or abbot might in fact receive episcopal consecration, but it was as prior or abbot, not as bishop, that he exercised authority over all persons, bishops included, within his community.

Columba had founded several monasteries, including Durrow and Derry, before leaving Ireland; but when in A.D. 563 he established his headquarters in Iona, and from then until the seat of authority was transferred to Kells in 814, the 'Columban Church' meant all the houses in Ireland and Scotland acknowledging the supremacy of the Abbots of Iona, the 'Coarbs of Calumcille' (heirs of St Columba). While it is most probable that Christianity had gained a footing in the South Isles before his time, it appears that the church in Islay soon became merged in the Columban order, as it undoubtedly was at the end of the 12th century.

As to the character of the ancient Celtic monastery, the best evidence naturally comes from Ireland. Bounded by a wall—commonly of earth and stone, but sometimes a rampart of great strength—the monks' cells and other edifices, both in the time of Columba and for long afterwards, were unpretentious architecturally. Plate 1 *a* gives some idea of a typical small religious community. The curve of the surviving section of the enclosure suggests that there might have been about 20 in this Church Island community of Co. Kerry, the buildings comprising monks' cells, guest accommodation, stores and other offices, school and chapel (or oratory). The cells were usually of the circular or oval beehive type, built in drystone with the walls continued corbel fashion to form the roof. Exceptional in structure was the chapel which was invariably rectangular in internal ground plan. Our illustration shews a normal oratory with small E window over the altar and the doorway in the W. These chapels were very small—anything from 12 to 25 ft. in length—and a large monastery might have several to meet its requirements. It appears from the literary evidence that the earliest of the Irish chapels were built of wood or wattle and clay, though in rocky, treeless parts of the country they would tend to have low drystone walls thatched with local material, and it is this latter type which has best survived the ravages of time.

So far we have been speaking of the typical 5th-6th century monastery for a small community. Those ruled by notable abbots or containing famous schools would be very much larger, but the large establishments would differ from the small ones only in the number of their buildings and not in the character or size of the structures themselves.

In Ireland the inevitable urge towards improvement brought a particularly interesting development in church architecture. The technique of corbelling was applied to the oratories as well as to the cells, and there are various examples revealing the nature of the methods initially employed—and also their severe limitations. Corbel roofing is appropriate to a building with circular walls; but when applied to a rectangular edifice the roof tends to sag and collapse inwards. The answer to this problem was ingenious. The external appearance of a high-pitched corbel roof was preserved; but beginning about halfway up the slope a strong inner roof of barrel vaulting was constructed in true arch formation. Thus reinforced, the outer roof was continued up to its completion. Besides propping the outer roof, the barrel vaulting formed the floor of a loft (or 'croft') which might or might not be used as a living or storage chamber.

It is interesting that what may be the earliest example of the use of the barrel vaulted propping arch is the oratory at Kells, Co. Meath (1 *b*), which is believed to be the church the completion of which in A.D. 814 allowed the monks of Iona to move their headquarters to Kells. From this 9th century style Irish ecclesiastical architecture gradually developed under various refining influences to its highest form, 'Irish Romanesque', in the 12th century.

These architectural developments, however, have no relation to the church history of Islay; and to correlate the Irish with our ancient ecclesiastical remains we have to refer back to the primitive monastic establishment. It must be admitted that, while monasteries are traditionally associated with various sites, including Nave Island, Kilchiaran, Nereabolls, Kildalton and Texa, such ecclesiastical remains as are readily apparent at these places are mediaeval. But if evidence of ancient occupation ever yields to archaeological investigation, we can with some degree of confidence predict what it will amount to. It will be related to the primitive Irish remains characteristic of the backward areas of that island and illustrated in Plate 1 *a*.

Though we cannot point to well preserved monastic sites in Islay, we do have numerous ancient chapels. Among the ancient chapels of Ireland there are some which, though of the same character as the monastic oratories, are 'secular' in the sense that they pertained to the establishment of some magnate or to a 'baile' or small township. Most of the ancient chapels in Islay are to be understood in the same way. They had thick drystone walls and, as a general rule, the roofs seem to have been thatched, resembling the early Irish monastic oratories on which they must have been modelled. In some few cases the sites plausibly suggest the retreats of hermits, but most of them are too closely associated with ancient settlements of the people to admit of this explanation. The most satisfactory theory so far advanced is that the chapels constituted a primitive anticipation of the parochial system. Each small district, it is presumed, built its own chapel and burial ground, custody being hereditary, perhaps, in a certain family. For the performance of all offices beyond the competence of the lay custodian a priest would attend from a neighbouring monastery.

It will be observed that the Irish oratories have the doorway in the W wall. (The oratory at Kells is no exception, for the present S doorway is modern, the old W one having been filled in.) In Islay the chapel at Kilslevan (II *a*) follows the Irish tradition, but at (*b*) Cil Eileagain, (*c*) Tokamol and (*d*) Gleann na Gaoithe the doorway is in the N wall. It will also be noted that, apart from a curious (presumably later) irregularity, the Kilslevan enclosure is roughly circular, while those of Cil Eileagain and Tokamol are approximately rectangular. Dr Ralegh Radford suggests that the circular enclosures are characteristic of the early Celtic period, the rectangular ones shewing Norse influence consequent upon the 9th century colonisation of the Hebrides. This may well be so. It is quite certain that the Norse colonists quickly adopted the Christian religion, and there is evidence in the Isle of Man that they maintained some of the old chapels or 'keills' and built new ones of the same type.

These tiny edifices were still the only 'churches' in the Hebrides while the Celtic church in Ireland was developing its distinctive ecclesiastical architecture, and they must have continued in use into the 11th or even the early 12th century until a proper parochial system was instituted within the bishopric of the Sudreys (i.e. the Diocese of the Isles with its cathedral in Man).

The Oldest Christian Monuments of Islay

Although the architecture of the Celtic church in the west of Scotland was rude by any standard, there was a much closer participation in the development of a universally renowned sculptural tradition.

The beginnings were, of course, modest. At monasteries, local chapels, burial grounds and open-air stations it was a general practice to set up a cross or crosses. Initially the idea of producing works of artistic merit would have had very little influence in comparison with the more basic urge to dedicate places and people and to enfold them within the peace of the Lord. Development of the art forms sprang from the desire to make the visible symbols worthy of their purpose.

This is not to say that stones of simple design or clumsy execution are necessarily earlier than those of more sophisticated conception and accomplished technique. Monumental styles of any place and time are significantly affected by the prevailing level of culture. Thus, even when themes are taken over by a primitive community from a more highly developed civilisation, the quality of the art may noticeably deteriorate. Again, work of a relatively high standard may be contemporary with or succeeded by crude imitation. There are, indeed, many reasons for distrusting any dating system based on the hypothesis 'The cruder, the earlier; the later, the better'; and this caution is necessary when dealing with the early Christian monuments of Islay. The island lay on the western fringe of civilisation. It had itself no tradition of creative art, and its sculpture represents the assimilation of motives, styles and techniques originating in the wider world of Christendom.

But all this having been said, we may nevertheless take it that, in a broad sense, the chronology of the ancient carved stones of Islay does in fact proceed from the simple to the more complex. Here early Christian influence was channelled mainly if not exclusively through Ireland and Iona; and the evangelists of the Celtic church were extremely ascetic in their whole mode of life until at least the middle of the 7th century. Ascetic puritanism is not normally associated with richness and variety in the fine arts, and all we know of the period indicates that it was a rigidly puritan scale of values that the missionaries brought to the west of Scotland. Hence all the earliest of our stones may be expected to shew a severe simplicity, though it does not follow that all the simple or crude examples must be early.

1. Rough-hewn Crosses and Incised Cross-slabs

Slabs with Simple Linear Crosses Only

Among the very earliest stones typologically are slabs or pillars with a linear cross made by 'pocking' with some kind of punch and hammer.

One of the decorative motives of the pagan world 'baptised' into Christianity was the 'Chi-Rho', formed thus: ☧ . It was specially acceptable because it could be interpreted as a monogram formed by the first two letters of Christ's name in Greek —'Chi' ('X', pronounced 'CH' as in 'loch') and 'Rho' ('P' pronounced as 'R'). In course of time the limbs of the 'X' closed to form a horizontal bar with expanded ends ⳩ and the gradual elimination of the loop of the 'P' resulted in an equal-armed cross, '+'. Crosses bearing traces of the original Chi-Rho are found both in Galloway and in Ireland. There are none in Islay, however, and the literary evidence would seem to indicate that the symbol had been completely displaced by the simple '+' by the time the Irish missionaries arrived in western Scotland. Thus in the *Life of St Columba* (522-597) Adamnan (628-704) tells us that the saint gently reproved a monk for not "imprinting the sign of the Lord's cross" (65b-66a) on a vessel before pouring in the milk. In dealing with the Loch (or River) Ness Monster he "raised his holy hand and drew the saving sign of the cross in the empty air" (75a); and the doors of King Brude's fortress miraculously opened after the saint's "imprinting the sign of the Lord's cross" upon them.

In these references it is clear that the cross is a vehicle of power. The making of the sign is the initiatory incident in a miraculous event, an efficacious invocation of divine grace. It may safely be assumed, therefore, that buildings and their precincts were by then dedicated and protected by incising crosses on parts of the structure or on a stone or stones erected near the entrance.

These passages in the *Life* do not, of course, prove that Columba used the sign. But Adamnan's belief that he did is pretty conclusive evidence that it was not an innovation in Adamnan's own lifetime, and he was born only thirty-one years after Columba's death.

Outline Cross-slabs and Rough-hewn Free Crosses

The outline cross incised on a slab (see III *b*) is probably contemporary with—and certainly cannot be earlier than—the free-standing cross of stone or wood.

There were free-standing wooden crosses by at least the early part of the 7th century. Writing, about the year 690, of a place at which Columba sat on the last day of his life, Adamnan says that a cross was later fixed there in a mill-stone. The mill-stone base indicates that we are dealing with a shafted cross, not a cross-slab; and as the mill-stone would be of the small handmill type, we may infer that the cross was of wood rather than of stone. Adamnan does not say when it was erected, but it may well have been before his own birth (628), for Bede (673-735) tells of a wooden cross set up by King Oswald of Northumbria before engaging in battle *c.* 635. Oswald had been educated in Iona, and presumably he had become familiar with wooden crosses in that island. Roughly shaped free-standing crosses in stone, such as Gleann na Gaoithe No. 73a (III *a*), may well have existed at this time in localities where wood was scarce; but the outline crosses on the slabs have the sharp angles of a wooden cross. These models, on the literary evidence, could be as early as the first part of the 7th century in Argyll and the Isles, and may well have been introduced with Christianity in the 6th century.

For Islay, then, it may be reasonable to assign the crudely formed stone cross and the two simplest forms of cross-slab (linear and outline cross-slabs) *typologically* to the 6th-8th centuries. This does not exclude any earlier date, nor does it imply that all existing examples were made so early. It only means that, on the general evidence, these stone crosses and slabs would have been characteristic of the earliest Christian centuries in Islay.

Of the examples shewn on Plate III, *a* (Gleann na Gaoithe No. 73a) is one of three stones found by Mrs Iain Ramsay at the ancient chapel in that glen in the Rhinns of Islay. About 18 in. high in its present condition (part of the shaft is apparently missing), it has been roughly trimmed to the form of a cross. The very simplicity of the monument precludes exact dating and it lacks any specific characteristics which might indicate its purpose. It has, however, a very strong resemblance to stones found in Ireland and may usefully be compared with grave-stones in the cemetery of the ancient Irish monastery of Skelig Michael.

Kildalton No. 79a (III *b*) is now in the National Museum of Antiquities, Edinburgh, but Mrs Iain Ramsay has a replica at Surnaig House. It is a small slab of local stone 2 ft. 2 in. long, and the outline cross was apparently made by 'pocking' with punch and hammer. It had been interred in the foundations of the High Cross at Kildalton, presumably when that monument was erected about A.D. 800, and was brought to light when Mrs Lucy Ramsay had the decaying foundations reconstructed. The manner of its preservation suggests that it was regarded with special veneration, and it may have been associated with the original establishment of the monastery on that site.

2. Carving in Relief

Excluding the two High Crosses of Kilnave and Kildalton, our ancient monuments carved in relief are all fairly small. We have no direct evidence as to when relief carving began in Islay, but the early 8th century is probable. This dating is suggested because the technique is later than that of incision, but must have been well advanced by the mid-8th century to which we shall assign the High Cross of Kilnave. Most of the stones in this class are 'ring-cross' slabs which will be discussed presently, but Plate III shews two ringless examples.

Kildalton No. 88 (III *c*) is a stone with undressed surface and poorly drawn cross in moderately high relief. It is closely related in style to one or two stones at Glendalough, Co. Wicklow.

Kilchoman No. 54 (*d*) exhibits work of a very different character. It is a good example of the 'two-' or 'three-in-one' found also in Ireland and Wales. Our stone shews (i) a roughly cruciform exterior, (ii) a Latin cross carved upon it in relief, and (iii) on the latter an incised linear cross with splayed terminals. It and Kilchoman No. 55 (see V *c*) are situated some distance from the churchyard and from each other and are called 'sanctuary crosses'. This presumably means that they, with others, marked the bounds of the 'peace' of the church there; but any tradition as to their precise function was already blurred when Graham was collecting his material in the last decade of the 19th century.

The 'three-in-one' stone under discussion has such a distinctive style that one feels it ought to be capable of reasonably definite dating. So far as its constituent motives taken separately are concerned—the roughly cruciform exterior, Latin cross in relief and incised linear cross with splayed terminals—there is no difficulty about assigning them to the early 8th century. But the distinctive character of the stone consists in their combination and neat execution. This is unique in Islay, and so evidence for dating must be sought in other regions of the British Isles. It may be added that the slab now lies prone in a field, slowly weathering away, and should as a matter of urgency be removed and placed inside Kilchoman Church.

3. The 'Celtic Ring' Crosses

The 'Celtic ring' cross (sometimes improperly called a 'wheel' cross, and so confused with a type quite different in character and local distribution) was widely used over Ireland, Argyll, the Isles and Scotland north of the Forth, varying in quality from the crudely incised slab to the magnificent monuments of Pictland and the High Crosses of Ireland and western Scotland.

The problem of dating even the most primitive looking examples is complicated by a major controversy over the origin of the ring. There is, of course, a form of ring cross the origin of which is not open to doubt. We have already noticed (p. 7) the development of the equal-armed cross from the Chi-Rho monogram. Sometimes this symbol was encircled in a ring representing the wreath of victory or 'glory', and this became the cross within a ring, '⊕'. Let us call this the 'monogrammatic ring-cross'. From it are derived the characteristic 'wheel crosses' of Galloway and adjacent districts.

As distinguished from this 'monogrammatic ring' completely enclosing the arms of the cross, there is the 'Celtic ring', encircling the crown but cut by the protruding arms and shaft. It is called the 'Celtic ring' because of a general assumption that it originated in Ireland; and the traditional view, held e.g. by Kermode (*Manx Crosses*, p. 13) and Nash-Williams (*Early Christian Monuments of Wales*), was that, like the wheel-cross of Galloway, the 'Celtic ring' cross developed from the monogrammatic ring.

But this traditional view has been challenged.

Alternative Theories of Irish Origin

Of the rival theories, three of the best known accept an Irish origin.

Origin on the Wooden Cross. The theory nearest to the traditional view is that the Celtic ring evolved on a wooden cross. Professor O Riordain suggested that, to ease the strain on the joint, stays or struts were fixed across the four angles, and that these would be shaped as quadrants of a circle so as to form a ring at the crown. This suggestion is not very plausible. No self-respecting carpenter worth his fee would so botch the job as to require strutting of his joint. He would simply cut a neat 'halved joint' locked with a wooden pin.

If the Celtic ring did in fact evolve on a wooden cross form, the process is more likely to have been something like this: Irish churchmen were familiar with the cross encircled in a 'glory'. To add a glory to a wooden shafted cross, the arms would have to overlie the ring so that arms and ring might be nailed together, and the shaft would be a prolongation of the lower limb (see lateral arms and shaft of V *c*). But to represent such a wooden ringed cross in an outline drawing or carving in stone, one would have to draw it as though the ring were actually cut by the arms and shaft, even though only the lower limb were shewn as extending beyond the ring to constitute a shaft. Once the encircling ring had been so represented as 'cut' by the overlying arms, an ever increasing process of unskilled draughtsmanship on the one hand, and imaginative artistry on the other, would take command. From this unplanned process of development there would eventually emerge the conception of the Celtic ring cross, so intrinsically attractive and infinitely variable in form as to have retained its appeal to this day.

On this theory of origin, Celtic ring-cross slabs may well have existed from the late 6th or early 7th century.

Origin in Pre-Christian Art. Dr Corcoran, noting that symbols now regarded as essentially Christian may be found among pagan decorative motives going back to the Bronze Age, thinks it perfectly possible that the Celtic ring-cross was an adaptation from pre Christian art. On this theory it might go back to the 5th century.

Origin in Classical Art. Dr Corcoran has also drawn my attention to a recent article by Miss Helen M. Roe containing an illustration of a disc-headed cross with protruding extremities. It is at Bobbio in north Italy and the type may well have inspired the Irish form. Miss Roe considers that by the earlier part of the 8th century the characteristic form of the Irish High Cross (see the Ahenny crosses, Plate IV *a* and *c*) had been fully attained.

Without attempting to discuss the merits of her suggestion in detail, we may note that direct influence from Italy or even the Middle East cannot be ruled out on historical grounds. In the year 633 or 634 (thirty years before the Synod of Whitby, it may be observed) the Celtic church of southern Ireland conformed to the Roman rite in the celebration of Easter. This decision was taken after the return of a delegation which had spent three years in Rome consulting with other branches of the church. It is said that the members of the delegation were lodged with a Greek, a Hebrew, a Scythian and an Egyptian. The 'Egyptian' presumably belonged to what we should now call the Coptic Church, a church in which the 'Celtic ring' is extensively used. The museum of the University of Addis Ababa has an interesting collection of crosses of this type; and though it seems that they are all modern or mediaeval, the present curator considers that they preserve an ancient tradition.

Theory of Pictish Origin

A view tentatively advanced by Mr R. B. K. Stevenson is that the Celtic ring was evolved in Pictland during the period which gave us the magnificent cross-slabs of that region. The suggestion is that, initially inspired from Northumbria and Ireland, the Pictish sculptors evolved their own characteristic style, some of the finest products being not later than the second half of the 8th century. Of special significance in this context are those slabs, such as Aberlemno No. 2 (Plate IV *b*), on which the semicircular armpits of the cross are completed into circles by the addition of semicircular mouldings, giving four circles round the crown of the cross. The Celtic ring, it is suggested, was produced by a modification of these supplementary mouldings. Viewed together, they gave the impression of a large single ring cut by the arms of the cross, and this impression was adopted as a conscious design on later slabs. The design then passed over to Iona and Ireland in the late 8th and early 9th centuries, the free-standing ringed crosses of those areas being produced by cutting away the background of the slab so as to leave the ringed cross in clear silhouette.

What this implies—and Stevenson accepts the implication—is that *all* the examples of the Celtic ringed cross in western Scotland and Ireland, from the famous high crosses down to the crudest incised cross-slab, are *subsequent* to the 8th century cross-slabs of Pictland. Obviously such a theory excludes all our small Islay examples, even the most artless, from the 6th-8th century period to which some of them might otherwise be assigned.

The Ring-Crosses of Islay

If we adopt Stevenson's theory, the position will be roughly this: the first Celtic ringed crosses in the west of Scotland were the great High Crosses of the 'Iona Group' inspired by the slabs of Pictland; and for Islay this means the High Cross of Kildalton. We put it at about A.D. 800. Hence all our slabs with Celtic ring crosses will be 9th century or later.

On any other theory of the origin of the ring, the dating is rather more complex. Some of the ring slabs can with reasonable confidence be classed as late, and these will be dealt with in the appropriate context; but there are several which would have some claim to be considered as of the 6th-8th century period.

Thus, the lines of the cross Gleann na Gaoithe No. 73b (Plate v *a*) are drawn as one would represent a simple wooden cross with an attached ring, and this stone could therefore (except on Stevenson's theory) be as early as the introduction of Christianity to the island.

The three fragments constituting Eilean Orsay No. 73d (Plate v *b*) were found by Mrs Iain Ramsay in that island off the Rhinns of Islay. Together they measure 20 in. maximum length. The lower limb of the cross cuts the ring to continue as a shaft, but there is not enough of the slab to shew the relation of the ring to the other arms which may or may not have protruded beyond it. There are crosslets under the lateral arms, and these may have been repeated in the upper angles—in the manner of an altar cross—but on this point we can only guess. The technique is rather primitive, and here again we might be dealing with 6th-8th century work.

Kilchoman No. 55 (v *c*) is the second of the 'sanctuary crosses' already referred to (p. 9). It is badly weathered and the workmanship does not appear to have been particularly good, but it could have been modelled on a wooden cross with attached ring. The upper part of the stone has been trimmed to form a margin round the ring. The upper limb protrudes, and the lower limb is continued as a shaft, but the lateral arms merely cut the ring and do not protrude beyond it. This stone could probably be classified by reference to slabs in Knapdale, Ireland and Wales.

Port Ellen Area No. 77 (v *d*) is of a very simple design surprisingly rare in Argyll and unique in Islay. Its closest affinities, so far as I am aware, are with the 7th-9th century cross-slabs of Wales. In our example the slab is of local stone, 2 ft. 3 in. long in its present condition. The equal-armed cross in relief stands clear of the surrounding ring. The workmanship is rough, having been done apparently by pocking. The stone originally stood at the old drystone church of Kilbride, near Port Ellen, but after various moves it has come to rest in the National Museum of Antiquities, Edinburgh. In the early 16th century the lands of Kilbride belonged to the chapel of the Virgin Mary of Texa Island, and it appears from one reading of a passage in Adamnan that there was a monastery in Texa during the lifetime of St Columba. Dedications to the Virgin are later than that period, and the association of Texa and the lands of Kilbride suggests that the religious foundation in Texa may have been dedicated originally to St Bridget, superseded by the Virgin when the Columban church finally fell before the tide of mediaeval Catholicism.

All the Islay monuments so far considered have been classed, tentatively, as 'early'. But it must be emphasised that, quite apart from the controversial position of the 'Celtic ring', we are not professing to put a date to any individual piece of sculpture. The term 'early' refers strictly to styles and not to specific stones. Primitive styles can persist in backward areas, or there may be reversion to basic forms when (as in Iona) some catastrophe sweeps away the superstructure of a culture. Again, styles may be sufficiently attractive to persist over the centuries. Hence, while some stones—e.g. Kildalton No. 79a—are known on circumstantial evidence to be genuinely early, others quite as simple in character may have been produced very much later.

4. The Ancient High Crosses

In astonishing contrast to the small slabs are the two high crosses of Kilnave and Kildalton.

(1) *The High Cross of Kilnave* (*c.* A.D. 750)

Though now broken and badly weathered, this cross, Kilnave No. 33 (VI *a*), was a very fine piece of sculpture in the Irish tradition. It stands about 8½ ft. high in the churchyard, and the sketch (VI *b*) shews what must have been the outline in its unbroken state. The carving is restricted to one face, but the skill and delicacy of execution are of a very high order. On a background of closely worked key-pattern and interlace there were five panels of spirals, viz.: a central medallion, two smaller ones in the lateral arms, and two rectangular panels (one on the upper limb, one on the shaft).

The spiral-work has a long history. It developed from a much simpler style of Bronze Age stone carving which may be seen at New Grange, and from the pre-Christian ornamentation in precious metal for which Ireland was famous. The inherited talent was later used in the service of the church for the embellishment of reliquaries and other sacred objects. One of the most beautiful examples is the early 8th century Ardagh Chalice which holds for us the additional interest that it has been adopted as a model for the Duncan Johnston and Margaret Duncan Memorial Trophies presented by the Glasgow Islay Association for award at the National Mod.

The varied motives in metal-work inspired many of the intricate and colourful designs found in religious MSS such as *The Book of Durrow* (Irish), the *Gospels of Lindisfarne* (Northumbrian) and *The Book of Kells* (probably begun in Iona though completed at Kells), these works dating from the late 7th century on, a period during which the associations of Northumbria, Iona and Ireland were particularly close.

When precisely the key, interlace and spiral patterns were first applied to stone is not perfectly clear; but if the elaborately carved ring-crosses of Ahenny,* Co. Tipperary, (IV *a* and *c*) are correctly dated by Dr Françoise Henry to the early 8th century, the sculptural phase in the golden age of Celtic art must have been initiated very soon after the literary.

Now the decoration of the Kilnave High Cross clearly belongs to the Irish tradition exemplified in the Ahenny crosses; and since we cannot seriously regard this as having evolved independently in Islay itself, we must suppose the Kilnave Cross to be the work of a sculptor trained in an Irish school. Hence we cannot put it before the early 8th century. At the same time, it is quite untouched by other traditions of

* When dating the Ahenny crosses it is probably correct to ignore the carved panels of the plinths. The figure carving on that of the North Cross (IV *c*) is surely later. We must also ignore the dreadfully degenerate panel of 'interlace' on the North Cross itself. Dating is also affected, of course, by the question as to the origin of the ring.

Central Scotland and Northumbria which profoundly modify the Irish characteristics of the Kildalton Cross. This suggests that Kilnave must be the earlier of the two; and as we shall find reason to date Kildalton to about the beginning of the 9th century, we shall probably be fairly near the mark if we assign Kilnave to *c.* 750.

Plate VII compares in skeleton form the designs in three of the Kilnave panels with kindred works. (i) The central medallion on the crown is much the same as designs in the *Book of Durrow* and the *Book of Kells*. (ii) The panel of the upper limb compares in general though not in detail with one on an early 10th century cross-shaft at Kells. (iii) The shaft panel seems to be exactly the same as the lowest panel of the High Cross of Keills in Knapdale which, taken as a whole, is intermediate as between Kilnave and Kildalton.

(2) *The High Cross of Kildalton* (*c.* A.D. 800)

Kildalton No. 79 belongs to what is called the 'Iona group' of which there are three reasonably well preserved examples: the St Martin's and St John's Crosses in Iona itself, and that of Kildalton (VIII). All are free-standing Celtic ring crosses and, despite some minor differences, of the same school. Kildalton is apparently the only one surviving in its entirety. St Martin's has slots at the ends of the lateral arms, suggesting that there were extensions which are now lost. St John's, composed of no less than seven pieces, has fallen apart on more than one occasion, and some of the original sections have not been recovered. Kildalton, made of a single block of local bluestone, stands in the churchyard 9 ft. high, weathered but unbroken. "The special feature of its character is the intense Celticism of its art. No other cross now standing exhibits this in such a striking manner. Its two panels, filled with divergent spirals and trumpet patterns, and mingled with circles enclosing groups of spirals, wherever they might be found and in whatever material they might be executed, would be certainly recognised as products of Celtic art. Nothing like them can be instanced among the art-products of any other people or any other time. I make such remarks as these with what may be regarded as needless iteration. But I do so because I wish to set clearly in the broad light of the present culture the important fact that many of these little regarded relics of the earlier culture of our country are worthy of attention for this reason, if for no other, that when they are gone there will be no more like them in the world—the species will be extinct. It does not seem as if we yet realised the fact that, as a nation, we are the sole possessors of a series of sculptured monuments unique in their character, and possessed of singular merit as works of art." (Joseph Anderson, *Scotland in Early Christian Times* (Second Series), p. 80.)

The dating of the 'Iona group' has been much disputed, and the reader interested in the details of the controversy is referred to the Bibliography on p. 60. The most judicious weighing of the aesthetic and historical evidence is that of Mr Stevenson who assigns the group to the early 9th century, and his view is the one here adopted.

Both in form and ornamentation the Kildalton cross, like the other members of the group, is a product of different traditions. As to *general form*, it can in the main, and without prejudice to the question of the ring's origin, be classed with the Irish ring crosses, though it is conceived on more graceful lines. This is largely due to the sweeping curves of the head, and it will be noted that a Northumbrian feature has been incorporated in the upper limb and lateral arms: the sides of the outermost sections are not straight but concave.

When we turn to the *ornamentation* we find a still more complex ancestry. On the EAST FACE (VIII *a*) we have, on the upper limb, two angels and, below them, David rending the jaws of the lion (pictorial sculpture common to Northumbria, Scotland and Ireland). Immediately below this are two birds feeding from a bunch of grapes (classical motive transmitted through Northumbria).

The crown has a ring of rope-moulding enclosing some simple interlace within which there is a great boss composed of the bodies of reptiles (apparently an import from Pictland).

On the lateral arms, at either side of the crown are panels of serpents with tails intertwined to form bosses (again from Pictland); and at the extremities are two figure panels, the one on the sinister side representing Abraham about to sacrifice Isaac.

At the top of the shaft we have another panel of serpents with interlaced tails. Below this is a panel shewing the Virgin and Child with attendant angels (derived through Northumbria), and finally a large panel of spiral-work of the same type, though not of the same particular design, as that on the Kilnave Cross (Irish).

On the WEST FACE (VIII *b*) the large central boss and the three on the upper limb and lateral arms are formed by the bodies of serpents, the foreparts of which fill the surrounding space of the panels. Round the crown are four lions—all of which have lost their heads. Below the lion at the top of the shaft is a panel of boss and spiral-work, the peculiar central 'bird's nest with three eggs' (as it has inevitably been called) being a feature common to the Iona group and the High Cross of Keills, Knapdale. The large double panel occupying the remainder of the shaft is composed of serpents with tails forming bosses.

This, no doubt, is a pedestrian account of the ornamentation, but it will serve to emphasise the three different traditions which have been so harmoniously synthesised in the crosses of the Iona group to produce a distinctive local type; and this is highly relevant to the problem of dating.

The history of Northumbria's political and ecclesiastical relations with Pictland, Dalriada and Ireland indicates pretty clearly the mid-8th century as the *earliest* period to which the Iona group can be assigned; and it is with regard to the *latest* possible date that controversy has been acute. One suggestion is that the group belongs to the 11th century, the substance of the argument being that these ring-crosses are derived from the 'wheel-cross' slabs of Man which are themselves alleged to be a 10th-11th century Anglo-Scandinavian creation. Despite the eminence of the principal advocate of this view, it can be summarily dismissed on straightforward aesthetic grounds. There is no need to derive the free-standing ring-cross from the Manx cross-slab when there are so many other more probable sources both in Ireland and in mainland Scotland. As to the decorative motives of the Iona group, they are in a world apart from the coarse, undisciplined vitality of Manx sculpture, and the spirals in particular belong to an older tradition of delicate craftsmanship which the Manxmen never attempted to master. We are not here comparing the relative merits of the two styles but simply asking whether we can, with any plausibility, derive the Iona type from the Manx; and the answer is, surely, 'No'.

If the 11th century suggestion is ruled out on aesthetic grounds, the 10th and greater part of the 9th must be rejected on historical grounds. This was the period of Norse colonisation and assimilation. While the available evidence indicates that the Celtic church maintained a continuous life in the Hebrides during this period, and that even vulnerable Iona was never completely deserted for any long interval, nevertheless it was abandoned from time to time, work on the illuminated MSS was apparently transferred to Kells, and the circumstances which rendered this expedient, and indeed dictated the permanent transfer of the headquarters to Kells in A.D. 814, were inimical to the island's remaining a great cultural centre. A simpler form of sculpture continued. There is, for example, the incised cross-slab illustrated in Drummond's Plate III which commemorates Abbot Flann who died in 891; but this stone is so simple in character that, were it not for the inscription, it might be attributed to a much earlier time. The existence of such stones argues relatively continuous occupation of the monastery, but it gives no support to the view that, subsequent to the removal of the headquarters to Kells, the remnant of the Iona community included a resident school capable of conceiving and executing the great high crosses.

Sometime between 750 and 814, therefore, must be the date of the Kildalton High Cross. It may be relevant to note that, when the foundations were being rebuilt in 1882 (see above, p. 8), the relics brought to light included, besides the incised cross-slab, some human remains. Judging by their condition, Sir Arthur Mitchell told Captain Ramsay that one of the persons concerned might have been put to the torture of the 'eagle'—a singularly unpleasant sport to which the Vikings were addicted.

Artistically as well as physically the crosses of Kilnave and Kildalton tower above everything else in the ancient sculpture of Islay. Though locally produced, they cannot have been produced by local craftsmen. The masons who made them must have been brought, in the former case, from one of the great Irish centres and, in the latter, from the community of Iona.

And they had no successors.

II

THE AGE OF THE GAEL-GALL

The story of Norse (or, as it is often improperly called, 'Danish') activity in the Hebrides is apt to be distorted. The early Viking raiders were no doubt ruthless, but speedily in the wake of the pirates came settlers, and Norse colonies had become established in the Isles and parts of Ireland by the middle of the 9th century. The Norwegians arrived as pagans, but from the very beginning their colonisation was characterised by intermarriage with the Celtic population and conversion to Christianity. Manx archaeology has shewn that the Gael-Gall—the mixed Celtic-Norse population—continued to build and maintain the ancient type of chapel, and we know from the Sagas that the converts 'raised crosses'. It is also true that, about the mid-10th century, an artistic revival spread over Man, Wales, western England, Galloway and eastern Ireland.

For some reason this revival failed to have any appreciable impact on the South Isles, but there are at least five stones in Islay which can be attributed to the Gael-Gall period. Four of them represent the continuation in some form of older Celtic tradition, while the fifth exhibits a definitely Scandinavian influence.

Kildalton No. 94 (not here illustrated) is a fragment of a slab the design of which is barely recognisable as part of an incised cross with hollow armpits and ring. It resembles some of the Iona stones of the 10th-11th centuries.

Laggan No. 32b (IX *d*) is a little slab found by Mr R. Hodkinson of Bowmore a year or two ago. The old chapel site and burial-ground are being gradually eroded by the River Laggan, and after a heavy flood Mr Hodkinson went to see whether anything had been exposed. He was rewarded by this interesting find which had been on a level some three feet below that of the mediaeval cross-shaft (XXXI *a*) to be referred to later. The slab, now 2 ft. 4 in. long, is badly broken so that the figure is incomplete, but the cross has a general resemblance to the 9th-11th century incised and inscribed slabs of Clonmacnoise and Iona.

There are, however, two unusual features. Firstly, the cross has two rings (not to be confused with the Celtic ring cross in a circular frame). I have not noticed this feature elsewhere except on a recumbent slab in Gigha (White's *Knapdale*, VI 3) and on some mediaeval stones such as the smaller Kildalton Cross (No. 80) and kindred recumbent slabs also at Kildalton. Secondly, the lateral arms completely overlap but do not protrude beyond the (outer) ring of the cross—the design in this respect resembling Kilchoman No. 55.

Gleann na Gaoithe No. 73c (IX *c*) is an undressed slab but full of interest. The principal device is a Celtic ring-cross with, near the foot of the shaft, a heavily cut cross-bar which presumably represents a base. On either side above the cross-head, and below it on the sinister (presumably also on the dexter) side are crosslets in semi-relief, all so clumsily cut that they are very difficult to identify. Almost at the top of the slab are two small cups which are perhaps irrelevant but may be intended to represent the sun and moon. The whole is a very badly executed piece of work, but the stone is easily classified because of the cross-head. The Celtic ring, the widely rounded armpits and the convex sides to the extremities of the arms presuppose the 'Iona group' of high crosses; and our slab is readily classed with the better examples of the type found in Iona and Ireland, especially at Clonmacnoise, some of which bear inscriptions dated to the 9th and 10th centuries. If this slab has always been at its present location it indicates that the chapel, or at least its burial-ground, continued in use well into the Gael-Gall period. Until it was recently moved the slab covered what Mr Bruce, an authority on Manx antiquities, suggested might be a 'lintel grave'.

Finlaggan No. 12a (IX *b*) was recently found at or near the ancient chapel (*Cil Eileagain* on older maps) at Balulive in the Finlaggan region. It is a quartzite boulder 15 in. long by 13 in. broad and is now probably much as it was when carved. The cross is composed of a single interwoven band. The ends of the lateral arms were made with a simple 'U' turn while the ends of the band itself remain open at the foot of the lower limb. The only adventurous exploit is the 3-loop summit of the upper limb. An incised crosslet will be noted above the arm on the dexter side, but there is no indication of any crosslet elsewhere. Stones of this type are sometimes called 'pillow stones', supposed to have been buried with the deceased, but this is a speculative issue. Our example is obviously related to similar cross-slabs in Iona and Ireland, and can be classed as 9th-11th century.

While the four examples just described derive from the ancient traditions of the west, there is one which belongs in a more intimate sense to the Gael-Gall period, namely the 'Doid Mhairi' cross-slab, Port Ellen Area No. 107 (IX *a*), now in the National Museum of Antiquities, Edinburgh. It is a roughly trimmed block of local stone 2 ft. 9 in. high, carved in relief, bearing a Celtic ring-cross with two circles above the arms (possibly representing sun and moon), and having rather odd flamboyant streamers rising from some exceedingly coarse interwoven bands. It is completely alien to everything else found in the island. At least one of the interwoven bands bifurcates, thus indicating a partly Scandinavian ancestry. A more exact description is given by Mr Stevenson (*PSAS*, 1958-59, p. 53) who classes the stone as late inferior 'Ringerike' of the latter part of the 11th century.

Those interested in the general history of the South Isles will note that this dating makes the stone contemporary with Godrod Crovan, King of Man and the Isles, who died in Islay *c.* 1093 and who is locally credited with the Bronze Age 'Carragh Bhan', near Kintra, as his memorial. The slab would also be roughly contemporary with the oldest part of the remains of Dunyveg (at Lagavulin); and it would have existed for over half a century before Somerled, ancestor of the Lords of the Isles, took the South Isles from his brother-in-law, the King of Man, and attached them to his dominions in Argyll. The Doid Mhairi slab probably marked the grave of an important Gael-Gall chief.

Mrs Lucy Ramsay's note on its discovery is recorded in *PSAS*, XVII, pp. 297-81:

> On the 30th January 1883, Donald McNab who had been in Mr Ramsay's employment for nearly fifty years took me to the spot where he found the slab about forty-five years before, and which was called 'Doid Mhairi'. It is situated in a large park about 300 yards west of Port Ellen distillery, and north of the limekiln which is on the side of the public road leading to Kintraw. I believe in a direct line it is nearly midway between the ruin and burying-ground of Kilnaughton and Tighcargaman,* where another cross once stood, the site of which is still to be seen.

* The spelling 'Tighcargaman' is a quite modern corruption of 'Tighcarmagan'.

Donald McNab describes 'Doid Mhairi' (previous to the date of finding the slab) as an uncultivated spot in the field about the size of a small potato plot or garden, on which a considerable quantity of stones lay, and there was some appearance of an enclosure or building having existed. The other parts of the field had been cultivated, but 'Doid Mhairi' had not, owing to a belief, as Donald McNab stated, that it might once have been a place of burial, from its resemblance to other places of burial in the district. It was, however, resolved to clear the spot, and while Donald McNab was removing the stones he found amongst them the slab now under notice. . . . 'Doid Mhairi' signifies in English 'Mary's Croft', meaning a small piece of ground such as a potato plot or small garden. No other object of interest, nor bones of any kind, were found at 'Doid Mhairi' or in any other part of the field when it was trenched or ploughed.

III

THE MEDIAEVAL STONES

Introductory

The Middle Ages opened in the Isles, it would be substantially true to say, in the latter part of the 12th century. The diocesan system of church government had been introduced in the early 11th, but for various reasons it was only nominally in force until about 1150 when the See of Man or the 'Sudreys' became a reality. The significance of the change appears in a papal document of 1203 which refers to 'the churches of Islay'; for it would appear that by 'churches' were meant, not monastic oratories or the local chapels, but edifices ranking as parish churches. Probably the E ends of the churches at Kilchiaran (Rhinns) and Kilnaughton (Oa) belong to that period.

There is still another reason for regarding this as the beginning of the Middle Ages in the Hebrides. In 1156 Somerled, petty king of Argyll, acquired the southern Sudreys, i.e. the Hebrides south of Ardnamurchan, commonly known as the 'South Isles' to distinguish them from the 'North Isles' on the far side of Ardnamurchan. It seems that he wished to detach his new acquisitions from the Bishopric as well as from the Kingdom of Man, for he tried to induce the then head of the Columban order, Bishop O'Brolchan, Abbot of Derry (where the headquarters had been moved from Kells), to re-establish Iona as the seat of authority. The offer must have been very tempting. Argyll was then a remote and inevitably neglected part of the diocese of Dunkeld; and the scheme must have been to unite Argyll and the South Isles under a single bishop who would in practice be effectively answerable only to the Pope.

But the attempt was unsuccessful. Under pressure from his primate (the Bishop of Armagh) and the High King of Ireland, O'Brolchan declined. The failure of Somerled's policy was catastrophic. His family turned their backs on the Columban church for ever and introduced the great mediaeval orders to their territories—Cistercians to Saddell and Ardchattan,

Benedictines to Iona.* The Benedictines were given all the rights and privileges of the old Columban church in the South Isles, and this gift included not only the Abbey Lands but also all the churches situated in Islay.

Among its many other effects, this change profoundly influenced the time and character of the sculptural renaissance in Argyll and the Isles. The typical mediaeval stones are not 'Celtic'. They have no ancestry in the ancient Scoto-Irish tradition. Though they are a distinct species, a unique West Highland and Hebridean product, the initial inspiration for their development came mainly from the monumental sculpture of northern England.

1. Recumbent Slabs: (A) Decorated in Low Relief

The mediaeval stones fall into two main groups: the recumbent slabs of various types and the free-standing crosses. The recumbent slabs of Islay are less varied than in mainland Argyll taken as a whole, and they may be conveniently divided into (A) those carved in low relief from which human figures are absent, and (B) those in which the effigies of warriors or churchmen are the principal content. We shall concentrate for the present on category (A), attending first to the slabs bearing a long-shafted cross with decorative head.

(1) *'Long-Cross and Foliage' Slabs*

Their Origin

Comparative study of the various types of slab in Class 'A' suggests that the primary form in Islay, and perhaps one of the earliest in Argyll generally, is the slab having a long-shafted cross with a decorative head, generally but not invariably accompanied by a sword on one side and a panel of scroll or foliage on the other (Plates XIII and XIV). Apart from two rather special and probably late examples at Kilmartin and Keills, Knapdale, these slabs are relatively few and apparently restricted to three localities, Iona (7 examples), Islay (5) and

* According to McVurich, a Clan Donald historian, the Benedictines were brought to Iona by Somerled's son Reginald. But on Somerled's death, Mull (and presumably therefore Iona) fell to the share of his eldest son Dugal. It may not be irrelevant to note that in 1175 Dugal became a benefactor and honorary brother of the Benedictine convent at Durham (A. O. Anderson, *Scottish Annals from English Chroniclers*, p. 264).

Kilmory of Knap (3). The design indicates northern English influence, and I shall explain what I consider this influence to have been, putting the theory in its most simple terms without the elaborations and qualifications which any authoritative writer on the subject would feel bound to include.

The view is this: both the *idea* of the 'long-cross and foliage' slab and also its *decorative motives* were derived from the carved stones of northern England. The idea was already embodied in such work as the slab at Kirkdale, North Riding of Yorkshire (X *a*), attributed by Collingwood (*Northumbrian Crosses*, p. 15) to the late 9th century. Colonel Cross has brought to my notice a tombstone from Jutland, now in the Danish National Museum at Copenhagen, dated to the first half of the 12th century, on which the arrangement of cross and scroll-work is similar to our own. The cross-head is unlike anything on our slabs, and the scroll-work is a much simplified version of the 'vine-scroll' of the Kirkdale slab; but the general conception is the same. This Scandinavian slab is probably English inspired; but however that may be, we in the west need look no further for the idea.

But a slab of the Kirkdale type could provide at most the initial suggestion. Its cross is of a solid, ancient pattern, and the scroll is a heavy derivative from classical vine-scroll, the total product being rather ponderous in comparison with the delicacy and vitality of our own examples. These finer characteristics, however, are themselves inspired by two other northern English sources, (i) a relatively plain Anglo-Norman slab with long-shafted cross, and (ii) pre-Norman Northumbrian variations on the vine-scroll.

(i) With regard to the first of these sources, we find the long-shafted cross in England (X) as early as the 12th century and very widespread in the 13th and 14th. The slab containing it, though sparsely ornamented as a general rule, may carry a few subsidiary designs, and one which is fairly common in the north is a sword lying parallel to the cross-shaft. This item also appears on a 13th century stone at Rushen, Isle of Man (X *c*). The general design, sometimes without but more often with the sword, became popular over Lowland and Central Scotland in the 14th century; and Paisley Abbey (XI *a*), Old Pentland, Midlothian (*b*), Fordoun, Kincardineshire, and Luss in Dunbartonshire are but a few of the localities in which it may be found. We can readily understand how the Iona (XIII *a* and *b*), Knapdale (*c* and *d*) and Islay (XIV) crosses could develop from such models.

(ii) Turning now to the scroll-work, we find that the Northumbrian masons of the 8th century produced a vine-scroll of great beauty which was succeeded in the 9th and 10th by variant forms (XII); and it was pretty obviously from these stones that our masons drew their inspiration when adding scroll patterns to the long-shafted cross.

To assign such an ancestry to the mediaeval sculpture of the West Highlands in no way detracts from its merits. Work of high aesthetic quality need not necessarily be 'original' in the sense of absolutely new creation. Its quality depends far more on the disciplined imagination with which it can develop themes already given. And such imagination was certainly in command in the present case. Neither with respect to the long-cross nor with respect to the scroll-work are the Highland slabs a mere combination of the original sources. The cross-heads take on a form of their own, and the vine-scroll (excepting a few cases such as the Knapdale piece on XIII *d*) is transformed into foliage.

Foliage of the West Highland Slabs

Of the Northumbrian vine-scroll, two designs form the basis of all our typical foliageous patterns.

The *first* is the column of heart- or pear-shaped grape clusters shewn in the central example of XII *a* and the left-hand examples of *b* and *c*. Our initial adaptation of this was apparently to transform the grape clusters into eliptical or heart-shaped foliageous designs of which there are various examples on XIII, XIV and XV. In this adaptation the clusters have become fleshy leaves. Sometimes we get a multi-lobed 'leaf' with twin stems, as in XIII *a*; sometimes even the suggestion of foliage is superseded by a merely stylised pattern as in XXII *a* and *b*. But normally the grape clusters are represented as a pair of leaves side by side or with their stems intertwined; and this, with minor differences of detail, is by far the most common pattern on the recumbent slabs.

The *second* of the Northumbrian designs, which we may call the 'single-stem serpentine', is shewn in the right-hand examples of XII *b* and *c* where a single stem produces grape clusters and subsidiary tendrils in its winding ascent. This has been incorporated more or less direct in the Knapdale scroll of XIII *d* while the most simple adaptation is the foliage of the long-cross slabs Iona XIII *b* (sinister panel) and Kildalton Nos. 89 and 99 (XIV *c* and *d*). This pattern, at first sight unpromising, will be met with later in some of the finest examples of mediaeval Islay carving.

Distribution and Dating

As already mentioned, the long-cross slabs of specifically West Highland type are comparatively few (a total of 15) and found only in Iona, Islay and Knapdale. Of the 7 Iona examples, 3 are very individual pieces of work and unhelpful for our purposes, but the other 4 form a closely related group sufficiently illustrated by XIII *a* and *b*.

All 3 of the Knapdale stones are shewn (XIII *c* and *d*; and XXII *c*), and it will be seen that only XIII *c* is nearly related to those of Iona.

Of the 5 Islay examples, 2 (Nos. 8 (XIV *a*) and 10) are at Finlaggan, 1 (No. 29 (XIV *b*)) is at Kilarow, and 2 (Nos. 89 and 99 (XIV *c* and *d*)) are at Kildalton. These are all clearly of the same class as the Iona group of 4, with the exception of No. 89 which has an unusual type of cross-head (compare Old Pentland stone, Plate XI). This minor variation must be significant, but it does not materially qualify the common character of the Iona and Islay work. At least 4 of the Islay slabs are by members of the Iona school, and all 8—4 Iona and 4 Islay—were probably made within a very short period, presumably by masons based on Iona. Graham thought that No. 99 was a late copy. His view was largely influenced by the excellent preservation of the stone. It is far more probable that it owes its good condition to having been covered for a long period. It is scarcely conceivable that any modern mason could or would produce such work.

It is very interesting that neither in Islay nor in Iona is there any trace of an apprentice hand practising long-cross slabs, nor is there any evidence of transitional forms as between the Anglo-Lowland and the Iona types. We have a few examples of superb craftsmanship in the execution of a completely formed style: and that is all. This must mean that someone, at some time, was able to induce a few men of acknowledged standing to bring their skills to Iona and revive its ancient fame as a centre of the sculptor's art.

Who were these men? We do not know. Where did they come from? We can make a reasonable guess. The mediaeval community of Iona was Benedictine and Dugal of Lorne had been associated with that order in Durham. It is in northern England that we find the Kirkdale slab. It is in northern England that we find the sword most commonly associated with the long-shafted cross and the varied forms of the vine-scroll from which our foliageous patterns have developed. There is therefore a strong presumption that the Benedictines of Iona were a colony introduced from the great convent at Durham by the sons of Somerled towards the end of the 12th century; and the probability is that, in course of time, the masons who carved our long-cross slabs were brought to Iona from the same centre.

As to when they are likely to have come to the west, the 14th century seems most probable. That is when the long-shafted cross became popular in Lowland Scotland, and there is nothing to suggest that the artistic revival in the west was of an earlier date. After 1314 the island of Mull and its satellites were given to Angus Oig of Islay on the forfeiture of the MacDugals of Lorne; and his son and heir, John, First Lord of the Isles, was known to the monks of Iona as 'Good John of Islay' because of his benefactions to the church. He is the person most likely to have been responsible for the sculptural revival, for only his reign (1329-80) provided the peace, wealth and patronage without which this new local art form could scarcely have developed.

The actual distribution of the long-cross slabs is of interest in this connection. The Knapdale area, containing Castle Sween which commanded the route to the north through the Sound of Jura, was of sufficient importance to attract magnates who, in the manner of the time, would be patrons of the church, but its long-cross slabs are not quite of the Iona type. Why should Islay not only share in the distinction of the exclusive long-cross style but be so much more closely connected than was Knapdale with the Abbey of Iona? No doubt Iona's strong vested interests in the churches and abbey lands of Islay would make for continuous contact. But probably the most important factor was that Islay contained the principal court of the Lordship of the Isles, the palace of Finlaggan—'palace', because it was not primarily a fortress but a residential mansion. It is significant that of the 5 Islay long-cross slabs, 2 are at Finlaggan. This strengthens the presumption that they belong to the reign of 'Good John'. It is on record that he had the domestic chapel repaired and furnished; and it was in his time that Islay reached the zenith of its importance, Finlaggan being then in reality as well as in name the principal court of the Lordship.

(2) *Classification of 'A' Slabs*

Leaving aside the long-cross slabs which are in a category by themselves, it may be asked whether any significant classification can be made of the other monuments in Class 'A'—i.e. the remaining recumbent stones decorated in low relief. Not much can be attempted in this respect until the survey of the Royal Commission on Ancient Monuments has been completed for Argyll. For Islay, however, it is possible to make a very broad tentative classification in point of style and an equally broad one chronologically.

Division in Terms of Foliage Style

(i) *Elliptical or Heart-shaped Foliage Design.* This pattern, already familiar to us in the long-cross slabs, is seen in typical arrangements on Plate xv. Graham was himself particularly interested in Keills No. 1 (xv *b*) because he thought it could be dated (the intrusive 'D M E 1707' at the top is irrelevant) by the closely resembling foliage of an inscribed stone in Iona (xv *c*). The Iona inscription runs, 'HIC IACET CORPUS ANGUSII FILII DOMINI ANGUSII MACDOMNILL DE ILA'—'HERE LIES THE BODY OF ANGUS SON OF LORD ANGUS MACDONALD OF ISLAY'. It was assumed that the stone marks the grave of Angus Oig (*d.* 1329), father of 'Good John', and that it therefore dated foliage of this type to the first half of the 14th century. Drummond doubted whether the first name in the inscription was 'Angus'. Dr Steer confirms the accepted reading 'Angus' but adds the following comment: "The lettering [on this stone] is one of only three examples of a rare form, the other two of which are dated to 1489 and *c.* 1500 respectively. It is not likely therefore that this is the gravestone of Angus Oig." The wording of the inscription is itself curious. Had the person in question been Angus Oig, Lord of Islay, son of Angus Mor, son of Donald, surely he would have been described as 'Lord Angus' and not merely 'son of Lord Angus'. Further the 'MACDOMNILL' is clearly a surname and not specifically the name of the grandfather. Had the actual grandfather been intended the wording would have been in some such form as 'filii Donaldi'. It would be consistent with the presumptive dating of the inscription if the stone were really a late 15th or early 16th century one commemorating a son, legitimate or illegitimate, of Angus Oig, Master of the Isles, son of John the 4th Lord. This Angus never succeeded, but he was frequently referred to as 'the young lord' or 'Lord Angus'. Hugh MacDonald, clan historian, calls him 'Angus Ogg MacDonald', and in the State Papers of the time he appears as 'Angusius de Ile' and 'Angusius, Comes, Magister Insularum'. If the stone does in fact commemorate a son of this Angus, making it late 15th century, and if the long-cross slabs are all 14th century, the presence of this kind of foliage is not of much assistance in the dating of particular slabs. It is indeed so widely employed over Argyll that it may have been in use for as long as there was any interest in foliageous designs.

Most, though not all of the Islay foliage of this type has been done by first rate craftsmen. But even at its best the design has serious limitations. The virtual self-sufficiency of each unit makes for an attractive single column of scroll, but it is too inflexible to be successfully employed over a broader area. Thus Kilnaughton No. 76 (XV *d*), like numerous examples in Iona, has been wrought with meticulous care but is rather monotonously repetitive.

(ii) '*Single-Stem Serpentine*.' This scroll, found in its simplest form on Knapdale (XIII *d*) and Kildalton No. 89 (XIV *c*), is eminently adaptable and was used on the best of the Islay slabs, most effectively perhaps on the shaft of the Kilchoman Cross. It has two principal varieties, the 'ring' and the 'open' forms.

The 'ring' form can be seen to advantage on Kilarow No. 23 and Nereabolls No. 72 (XVI *a* and *b*). Though the surface of No. 23 is badly worn, we can see that on the dexter side of the sword the scroll is of the familiar elliptical or heart-shaped pattern, while on the sinister side it is quite different. At a casual glance it appears to consist of a column of rings enclosing foliage. But in fact none of the 'rings' is completely closed. What we have is a single stem throwing off a number of subsidiary ones in its winding ascent.

The plan is clearer on the beautiful and unfortunately broken No. 72 where the column on the sinister side has five 'rings'. Counting from the bottom, the first and third enclose a group of four trefoils; the second and fourth have three divided 'trumpet' leaves; the fifth—a less well preserved one—seems to have three trefoils with interwoven stems. On the dexter side of this same slab we have a good instance of the 'open' form of serpentine. There is a particularly fine example on Kilchoman No. 41 (XVI *c*) while Nereabolls No. 73 (*d*) is skilfully carved but degenerate in style.

Of course the merits of these slabs are only partially dependent on the use of single-stem serpentine with its potential versatility; for in some examples of its use, e.g. Kilarow Nos. 20 and 30 (XVII *a* and *b*), the scroll itself is rather decadent and unimpressive, the quality of the slabs depending on their overall merits—substandard in some respects, with other features to redress the balance.

Chronological Division

The last mentioned examples, Nos. 20 and 30, bring us to the question of dating. There is not much we can say under this heading. Certain slabs can, for various reasons, be assigned to particular times, but for general classificatory purposes there is only one very broad distinction we can at present draw: certain stones have characteristics which place them in the 16th century rather than earlier, and this enables us to assign —though very tentatively—some others to an earlier period.

Nos. 20 and 30 may with reasonable assurance be assigned to the 16th century. In this type we have a long central sword flanked by foliage panels and animal forms, the whole usually though not invariably surmounted by an elaborately decorative cross-head. The dating clues are found in (i) the form of sword-hilt, (ii) type of cross-head, and (iii) the comparative merits of foliageous scroll and animal forms.

(i) *Swords*. It will be noted that in all the swords of the long-cross slabs the quillons of the guard are short and thick with a pronounced downward curve, and the lobes of the pommel are short and splayed at a fairly obtuse angle. The sword, in fact, is rather like the illustration of a Viking or Anglo-Saxon weapon. It does not in the least follow that swords of that type were still in use when the long-cross slabs were made. They may have been, but memorials did not always adhere to contemporary weapons and dress. The fact is simply that on the long-cross slabs swords were drawn in that fashion. But in later slabs the swords are of the 'hand-and-a-half' or 'claymore' type, the quillons long and slender, and not curved but either straight or depressed at an angle. Where the pommel still retains lobes, these are more upright and delicately formed. In two cases, Nos. 20 and 30, the quillons have the four-ring terminals which, one understands, did not appear in the west of Scotland before the early 16th century.

(ii) *Cross-heads.* On the long-cross slabs the cross-heads are primarily geometrical figures tending to foliage at the extremities. On the group we are now considering the cross-heads, excepting No. 23 (XVI *a*) which belongs to neither class, are primarily foliageous, sternly disciplined by the requirements of symmetry. No. 30 is of particular interest because it is almost exactly the same as some Iona examples which can be definitely dated to the beginning of the 16th century.

(iii) *Foliage and Animal Forms.* One of the curious facts about the stones of Argyll in general is that the finest foliageous scroll is not contemporary with the most successful delineation of animal forms. With the best scroll work the animals tend not to be particularly well drawn; but later, the centre of interest apparently shifting, the animals acquire grace and vitality while the scroll becomes very artificial or frankly careless. These changes are particularly marked in some stones at Keills, Knapdale and Iona; and they are to some degree evident in Islay in the differences between Nos. 23 and 72 (XVI *a* and *b*) on the one hand, and Nos. 20 and 30 (XVII *a* and *b*) on the other.

While we cannot use these clues to date all the Islay slabs of Class 'A', they do assist in making a threefold division in accordance with which some of the stones can be distinguished. Thus to the 14th century can be assigned the long-cross slabs. To the 15th—and most probably to the late 15th—we may safely assign Kilarow 23, Kilchoman 41 and Nereabolls 72 as representative of the finest period of slab carving. To the 16th century can be attributed Nos. 20 and 30.

(3) *Slabs of Special Interest*

While the stones on Plates XIII to XVII *a* and *b* illustrate types, those on XVII *c* and *d* to XXII are chosen for their individual interest.

Kilchoman No. 40 (XVII *c*) with well cut but somewhat degenerate scroll, probably late 15th century, is of interest because of the additions made in the late 17th. It has evidently won the approval of a Campbell family who added the date '1678', the initials 'D.C.', and the Campbell gyronny-of-eight and galley of Lorn. There must have been some pretension to descent from the house of Argyll, direct or through Calder. Such appropriations of older stones were not uncommon. We find the same liberties taken with memorial 'brasses' in England, and attempts to preserve the priceless monuments in our West Highland churchyards are often frustrated by claimants whose titles are no better than can be acquired by robbery from nameless mediaeval graves.

Kilarow No. 16 (XVII *d*) has been more radically altered. The worn date at the top seems to be '1618', but, as Graham noted, the foliage on the sinister side at least is much older. The 17th century rapier would accord with the ostensible date, but Dr Steer suspects that the hilt of the original sword has been altered. Indeed the upper third of the slab seems to have been cleared and recut.

The border (not shewn) carries an inscription 'HEER LYES THE CHILDREN OF DAVID FRASER VIZ JAMES DANIEL CHARLES MARY SIMON AND JEAN DUFF HIS WYF'. We may take it that this Fraser family had been brought down from the north by Campbell of Calder after he acquired Islay in 1614-15; and if the date at the top is really '1618' and not '1648', death must have taken speedy and heavy toll. But apparently the line was continued, for we find a David Fraser and his son David at Skerrols, and a John who had the 'tuck milne' at Kilarow, all in 1686. Charles, surgeon, was in Gartahossen in 1741; and William, surgeon, was in Kilarow in 1738.

Nereabolls No. 70 (XVIII *c*), intended to represent the Evangelist's simile of the 'Vine and Branches', bears striking testimony to the way in which design may alter in transit over areas which have no acquaintance with the object represented. *a* is a 14th century example at Hexham, Northumberland, with recognisable grapes and leaves. *b* is an Iona one where the leaves have become nondescript. In the Islay example, *c*, they are more like oak than anything else, and the grapes have all fallen by the way.

Nereabolls No. 71 (XIX *a*) is conspicuous for the resemblance of some items in its decoration to those of stones in Kintyre. This applies to the panel of interlace and to the stag and hounds, but most especially to the representation (on the dexter side of the sword-hilt) of two animals in conflict. This is almost identical with a pair at the bottom of a McEachran cross-shaft at Campbeltown (XIX *b*) and one at Saddell. The Islay slab must surely be later than the two crosses of Kintyre.

Nereabolls No. 72, already discussed in another context (pp. 31-33), bears a very close resemblance to a slab in Oransay. The Priory, which was founded there by 'Good John' about 1350 for the Augustinians, had lands in Islay, but Nereabolls pertained to the Monastery of Derry in Ulster.* It may be inferred from this that the masons who carved the slabs did not necessarily work exclusively for any one community or even for any one religious order.

In 1963 members of the Islay Archaeological Survey Group located and subsequently reburied a slab at Kilnaughton which was not known to Graham and is now listed as 'Kilnaughton 76a'. Through the courtesy of Miss Marion Bennett and Dr Francis Celoria I have seen the photographs. Though part of the face has been damaged, this is a fine stone with a characteristic 15th century foliageous cross-head, central sword, and panels of single-stem serpentine scroll.

* In an interesting volume on *Tartans*, Lady Hesketh writes (p. 13): "In Islay, from 1587 onward, the annual ground rent payable to the Crown consisted of sixty ells of black, white and green cloth. Now the lands in question belonged during that time, except for one brief period, to the Macleans, and it cannot be entirely coincidental that to this day the Maclean tartan is made of the same three colours."

Lady Hesketh must be referring to the terms of a charter to Maclean of Duart in 1587. The Macleans never had Islay though they did hold lands there at various periods, as did many vassals of the Lordship of the Isles. And the only holding in the island which paid a rent in black, white and grey (*not* green) cloth was the 40/- land of Nereabolls. As already mentioned, this land belonged to Derry, and the old annual *reddendo* was 'sixty ells (or yards) of cloth, of white, black and grey colours respectively, or 8d in money prescribed for each ell'.

About 1498 the lands of the Abbey of Iona and the Islay lands of the Monastery of Derry were annexed to the Bishopric of the Isles, and shortly afterwards Nereabolls, with some other lands, was given in feu charter by the bishop to Maclean of Duart. In 1560, at the Reformation, these churchlands were taken over by the Crown; and in 1587 James VI renewed the feu charter on the old terms in favour of Maclean's grandson.

Three slabs at Kildalton, all having the 'ring-and-saltire' design found on the E side of the mediaeval cross there, are closely linked to the sculptured stones of Knapdale.

The *first* of these, No. 91 (xx *b*) is very worn, but one can see that the design was simple.

The *second*, No. 98 (xx *c* and xxi *a*), is unusual in having no foliage. Its ring-and-saltire has a certain resemblance to a slab at Keills, Knapdale (xxi *b* and xxii *b*), and the whole ring pattern of the upper half is almost identical with one (turned upside down) on the MacMillan Cross at Kilmory of Knap (xxi *c*). The otter pursuing a fish (sinister side of sword-blade) occurs nowhere else in Islay, but it is fairly common in Kintyre and Knapdale, and is found on one stone (bearing some relation to those of Knapdale) at Oransay Priory. This item may derive from an illustration of Scandinavian mythology found on a Manx slab (xxi *d*) shewing Loki about to cast a stone at Ottar who is out salmon-fishing; but if this is the derivation it was probably unknown to the carvers of the Argyllshire stones. Of course the motive may have a much older source, for we find something like it in the *Book of Kells*. Or, as Colonel Cross has suggested, it may simply be a representation of wild life.

The *third* stone, No. 100 (xx *d* and xxii *a*), has a type of scroll on the sinister side of the sword-blade which is very untypical of Islay work but exactly the same as that on a Keills, Knapdale, slab already mentioned (xxii *b*). Note also the dog-like animal at the bottom of the Keills slab which is practically the same as the one on the sinister side of the sword-hilt in No. 100. The figure on the dexter side of the sword-blade is unique in Islay, but it occurs twice at Kilmory of Knap (xiii *d* and xxii *c*) and once in a diminutive form at Keills. Its origin and significance are very mysterious.

The close relationship between the Kildalton and Knapdale work argues some family association, and the three ring-and-saltire slabs are probably MacNeill stones. The MacNeills of Gigha and Knapdale, sometime constables of Castle Sween under the Lords of the Isles, held the lands of Knockronisdail, Ardimersay and Ardilistry (in Kildalton parish) until these were sold to James MacDonald of Dunyveg in 1553-4.

(4) *Decoration of the Slabs*

Crosses, foliage and swords have already been discussed, and we shall merely add brief comments on some of the other main motives.

Shears. A common object was a pair of shears (e.g. very foot of xxii *a*). They are said to represent a woman, but we must treat this assertion with some caution since slabs with inscriptions do not always support the theory. Possibly this was the original significance of the shears (though we cannot really rule out the idea that they signified the cutting of the lifeline); but once an object became familiar, there would be a strong tendency to copy it on later stones merely as a decorative device.

The Galley. This is one of the most familiar objects. It may occur in simple outline form or in the elaborate manner of xix *a* where we have the large sail furled, a figure in the bow, another in the after riggings, flag flying and a shield hoisted in the stern. Here again we must avoid reading too much into the presence of the galley on a monument. We are told that Godrod Crovan bore a galley on the obverse of his seal, and that the same device was used by Reginald, son of Somerled. When armorial bearings were formally adopted, the galley was incorporated in the arms of the leading families of western Argyll and the Isles; but we are at liberty to doubt whether its appearance on our slabs would always have been sanctioned by a fastidious Lord Lyon King of Arms.

Horse and Rider. This popular motive does not occur on any of the Islay slabs but we have it on three of our cross-shafts (xxxi *c*, xxxiii and xxxv). It was apparently borne on the reverse of the seals of Godrod Crovan and Reginald, son of Somerled. This may or may not have popularised the motive in the west, but it is well to bear in mind that riders and cavalcades are familiar on the stones of Pictland.

Animal Forms. Of these there is a considerable variety. 'Paired beasts' from whose tails patterns of interlace proceed were common in ancient times. They occur on the high crosses of St Martin, Iona, and Keills, Knapdale, and they may have come to the west from Northumbria. They are also found on the mediaeval slabs and cross-shafts where their tails have gone over to the production of foliage.

More novel for the west of Scotland are the 'hunting scenes' (xix *a* and xxxi *b*) depicting stags and hounds which probably derive from Pictland. Some are well done, but all are pretty obviously drawn to conventional patterns, as may be seen if one compares the examples found over Argyll and the Isles as a whole.

Then there are the mythical animals, especially dragons and griffons (e.g. XVII *a* and *b*). These, again, are mere routine copies; but it is interesting to note the increasing skill in the carving of animal forms.

2. Recumbent Slabs: (B) Effigies

(1) *Warrior Effigies*

Another type of slab characteristic of Argyll and the South Isles is that of the warrior in very high relief. In Islay (XXIII) they are monotonous in conception and poor in execution. The figure occupies the full length of the slab. The protective armour consists of the following items: a high-ridged helmet (the 'bascinet') to which is attached a chain- or ring-mail curtain ('camail') covering cheeks, throat and shoulders and coming to a point over the breast; and a long coat-like garment (sometimes mistaken for the kilt) which is apparently the 'gambeson', made of stout material padded with wool in vertical lines, and sometimes worn over a mail shirt. A great sword is carried obliquely in front of the body, the left hand supporting it by the scabbard while the right grasps the 'fall' of the sword-belt.

Outside Islay the stones shew a little more variety. Thus, while Kintyre has some slabs virtually the same as the Islay ones, it has a few with a higher standard of workmanship and variety of treatment. In the example at Killean (XXIV *a*), possibly a MacDonald of Largie, the right hand grasps a ghostly spear—the carver having forgotten to include the material one—while the left holds an armorially charged shield. In various localities, and especially in mid-Argyll, the effigy frequently occupies only a part—at times a modest part—of the slab.

(2) *Relation to Lowland and English Effigies and 'Brasses'*

The best examples of West Highland warrior effigies are found in Iona, and two of these help to link the West Highland type with those of Lowland Scotland and England. One of them which, for some undisclosed reason, Drummond calls 'MacLean of Duart' is shewn on XXIV *b*. The pose is the same as that of the Killean figure but the dress is different. The

Iona warrior wears, not the quilted 'gambeson', but the light surcoat (presumably over chain mail), and he has a dog at his feet. Compare this with the 13th century English 'brass' of Sir John D'Abernoun (*c*).

(3) *Dating of the Islay Effigies*

These comparisons are suggestive when we try to determine the period of the West Highland warrior slabs. The 'bascinet' and 'camail' characteristic of our stones appear to have been introduced in England about 1330. The 'gambeson' was popular there between 1325 and 1335. The somewhat puzzling position of the right hand on the Islay slabs is made intelligible by the 'two-point' suspension of the sword shewn on XXIV *a* and *c*. The sword-belt is attached to a point near the top of the scabbard, passing round the body to meet the scabbard again at a point lower down. On the English brass here shewn, the 'fall' or free end of the belt is tucked behind the scabbard; but in all the Islay examples, as well as in many of mainland Argyll, it is grasped by the right hand of the warrior. In England, we are told, this method of girding on the sword belonged to the period 1250-1330.

Taking all these datings together, we can safely conclude that our West Highland warrior slabs cannot be earlier than 1330; and they are almost certainly considerably later. It would take some time for these monumental fashions to reach the west and assume their local form; and the representation of armour was, in any case, apt to be conservative. A person might be shewn dressed in the style of one or even two centuries before his own time. We have clear evidence of this in Iona where one of the figures on the slab commemorating John MacIan of Ardnamurchan (XXV *c*), killed in 1519, still retains the familiar garb. We are not likely to be far wrong, then, if we assign the Islay group to the 15th century.

The Islay effigies of this routine type are very few in number: Finlaggan No. 3; Kilarow Nos. 18 and 21; Kilnaughton No. 74; Kildalton No. 86—a total of 5 for the island. This and their poor quality suggests that they were all executed over a fairly short period by inferior craftsmen.

(4) *Slabs of Special Interest*

Finlaggan No. 3 (XXIII *b*) is interesting on account of its inscription which, though now suffering from exposure, was quite legible in Graham's day. It runs 'HIC JA(CE)T DONALDUS FILIUS PATRICI CELESTINI'. As 'Celestine' was the Latin rendering of 'Gilleasbuig', the translation is 'HERE LIES DONALD SON OF PATRICK SON OF CELESTINE (or if the last is a surname, MACGILLEASBUIG)'. It has been surmised that this stone may commemorate a grandson of Celestine, Lord of Lochalsh, son of Alexander, 3rd Lord of the Isles; but there is no tradition that Celestine of Lochalsh had a son named Patrick; and while the galley at the foot of the slab suggests, it does not necessarily indicate membership of a noble Hebridean family. More probably the slab marked the grave of a person of local standing. In 1541 the lands of Finlaggan, Staonsha and Balulive were held by Donald McGillaspy (i.e. MacGilleasbuig) who was accepted by the Crown Commissioners as representative of 'the old possessors'. The stone may commemorate a member of this family.

Kildalton No. 90 (XXV *a*) is in a quite different style from all the others. It lies within the ruins of Kildalton mediaeval church, a slab in low relief with a later type of pommel on the sword-hilt and some minor differences in the arrangements of the hands and sword suspension. A feature rare in Islay but common elsewhere is that the head rests on a pillow. Graham thought that the inscription might be 'HIC JACET ALAN SORLETI MACIAIN'—'HERE LIES ALAN SON OF SOMERLED MACIAN'.

This would pretty well identify him as a grandson of the famous—or, in MacDonald eyes, infamous—John MacIan of Ardnamurchan. MacIan had married into the house of Argyll and was the principal government agent in bringing the MacDonalds of Dunyveg to judgment for their rebellion in 1494. Already bailie of Islay under the last Lord of the Isles and holding certain lands there in virtue of that office, he was given most of the remainder of the island on the forfeiture of the MacDonalds of Dunyveg. He was slain in 1519 by MacDonald of Lochalsh, and his estates passed by a tortuous process to the Crown, but several members of the family were settled in Islay. His daughter Katherine had married Alexander MacDonald of Dunyveg who had been reinstated in a portion of Islay, and she was living at Bailenaughton Mor in 1541 with her second husband, John MacKay. In the same year, a MacIan held Stremnish and Bailechatrigan; Ian

MacIan in Kintour and Tallant helped to compile the Crown Rental; and Alaster, apparently the eldest son of the late John, held Proaig along with some other properties.

As John MacIan did have a son, Somerled, there is a strong probability that the stone refers to a grandson. Its late date —mid 16th century—would account for its divergence from the other effigies. 'Alan' does not sound like a MacIan name; and as the inscription is badly worn, this could be a misreading of 'Ian'.

Kildalton No. 101 (XXV *b*) is the only one of its kind in Islay though there are a few similar stones elsewhere. The one to which it is most closely related is the memorial to the above-mentioned John MacIan in Iona (XXV *c*). The MacIan stone was made to the order of his sister Mariota, wife of MacFie of Colonsay, and must have been carved very shortly after 1519, confirming the late date of West Highland slabs with inscriptions running round the borders, divided by rosettes. Despite the appearance of two figures under a double canopy, the Iona stone is for MacIan alone. In the Islay example it will be noted that one figure bears a sword and the other a mace over his shoulder; and so the effigies may represent the deceased in two capacities. His identity, however, is unknown, for the inscription has almost entirely disappeared.

(5) *Ecclesiastics*

Though warrior effigies are absent from the Rhinns, churchmen are well represented. Of the 9 listed examples for the whole of Islay, 5 are in the Rhinns, 3 at Kilarow, and 1 in the parish of Kildalton. This last mentioned stone, Texa No. 102 (XXVI *c*), is now in the National Museum of Antiquities, Edinburgh. The arrangement of the inscription round the border suggests a 16th century date.

Of those in Kilarow and the Rhinns, the three illustrations are sufficiently representative. On Nereabolls No. 69 (XXVI *a*) we have a foliageous cross-head, the figure of a priest in a niche with a chalice over his right shoulder, and on the lower part of the slab some single-stem serpentine proceeding from the tails of a griffon and another animal. On Kilarow No. 17 (*b*) the contents are much the same though differently arranged —the priest in his niche with chalice and remains of an inscription over his right shoulder; and below, a foliageous cross-head with some single-stem serpentine. If we have correctly dated such cross-heads in our discussion of the slabs decorated in low relief, these clerical monuments will all belong to the late 15th or early 16th century.

On Kilchoman No. 35 (*d*) the effigy occupies a considerably larger portion of the stone. According to local tradition it marks the grave of Maclean of Duart who was defeated and slain at the battle of Gruinard in 1598. The slab was, in fact, made for a churchman of an earlier period, but this does not tell decisively against the local tradition. Old stones certainly were appropriated for later burials.

Our ecclesiastical slabs are closely related to those of Kintyre.

3. The Mediaeval Crosses

Islay was unusually rich in mediaeval crosses, for although only two are now intact, the known fragments indicate that there were at least 12: 1 at Keills (Port Askaig), 1 at Kildalton, 2 at Kilarow, 1 in the Laggan district, 1 in Texa, and 6 in the Rhinns. Besides these, there are two Islay cross-heads in the National Museum of Antiquities but there is no record of the localities from which they came.

The crosses fall into two distinct groups: (1) Those devoid of human figures, having their heads decorated with geometrical designs and their shafts either plain or covered by simple foliageous scroll; and (2) the better known disc-headed crosses displaying the Crucifixion and often elaborately decorated with figures and foliage.

(1) *Crosses with Geometrically Patterned Heads*

(i) In this class should probably be reckoned Keills No. 2 (XXVII *a*) which now survives only as a broken shaft. The shaft so closely resembles one at Keills, Morvern (*b*), that the head was probably also of the same character.

(ii) Kildalton No. 80 (XXVIII *a* and XXIX *a*) is one of the two unbroken mediaeval crosses. It stands on a cairn base some 50 yards NE of the churchyard and is sometimes referred to as 'the thief's cross', presumably because, being outside the present churchyard, it is thought to mark the grave of some anonymous reprobate. It is, in fact, a fine piece of work. The decoration on the E face follows a pattern characteristic of 10th-11th century Manx slabs—a late Manx example is shewn on XXVIII *b*—which consists of two bands rising from the shaft and two from the lateral arms, the pairs being interwoven with each other and with one or more rings. The Manx example here illustrated carries the 'ring-and-saltire' motive of the Kildalton cross-head on its upper limb.

But any Manx influence which there may have been must have been distant and subdued. Certainly our cross cannot be classed with the 10th-12th century sculpture of Man. It is a free-standing cross, not a cross-slab; the overall design is severe and neatly executed; and the W face is in a different style.

The W face is, in fact, intermediate as between the E face and the cross-head of Keills, Morvern; and Colonel Cross has suggested that one of the main differences between the two stones may be accidental. The shaft of Kildalton 80 is absolutely plain except for the roll-mouldings at each edge; but this may mean that the work is unfinished. Had the shaft been carved like that of Keills, the two crosses might be included in the same general category.

(iii) Kilarow No. 28 obviously falls within this group. It is merely part of a cross-head, but it is sufficient, together with Graham's description of a fragment of the shaft, to enable us to reconstruct the cross (XXIX *b*) as it originally stood.

(iv) 'Islay' No. 108 (XXIX *c*) is part of a cross-head included among the stones presented to the National Museum of Antiquities by Captain Ramsay in 1922. It was apparently unknown to Graham, and was perhaps discovered after the publication of his book. There is no indication as to the part of Islay in which it was found. The exterior shape of the cross-head is unusual for the island and seems most closely related to late Anglian or Anglo-Scandinavian cross-heads, e.g. one at Irton, W. Cumberland. The decoration is also unusual—a cross-crosslet formed of interwoven bands on one side, and apparently repeated on the other, though in the latter case the pattern is almost entirely worn away. The nearest approach to this style of cross formation in our area is, I think, on one of the curious Iona 'long-cross' slabs (Drummond, Plate XXVII, 2).

It is most probable that the stones of this group represent the earlier type of mediaeval cross in Islay. Though the heads have their own individuality, they are all clearly of a family distinct from the ancient high crosses, on the one hand, and from the well known disc-headed crosses (Campbeltown, Kilchoman, Oransay, etc.), on the other. Their style tends to support the view, already advanced when discussing the long-cross slabs (see pp. 25-28), that the sculptural renaissance of our region drew its inspiration from northern England. This would sufficiently account for the suggestion of Manx characteristics in the E side of Kildalton 80; for the northern English cross-heads to which our group is most akin are, according to Collingwood, Anglo-Scandinavian.

(2) *Disc-headed Crosses*

(v) It will be convenient to begin with 'Islay' No. 109 (XXX *a* and *b*), another cross-head remnant presented to the Museum by Captain Ramsay. Here again, the locality in which it was found is not stated; but badly worn as it is, we have no difficulty in recognising the familiar disc-head. The representation of the Crucifixion seems to have been rather like that of Nereabolls No. 62 (XXXIII), except that the head droops to the right in a well known attitude.

This fragment is briefly discussed by Mr J. S. Richardson (sometime Keeper of the Museum) on p. 150 of *PSAS*, LXI (1926-27). The design has almost completely vanished from the back and its original character is uncertain, but the remaining traces suggest a foliageous cross-head as on Nos. 52 and 62 (XXXII and XXXIII). The description recording the gift (*PSAS*, LVII (1922-23), pp. 94-96) refers to this as "a cross with circles at the intersection of the arms".

(vi) Texa Nos. 103 and 104 (XXX *c*) are noted by Graham as figures on the plinth of the Texa cross-shaft No. 105. In Mr Richardson's notes just referred to he explains that this plinth was, in fact, a cross-head (apparently unfinished), the two figures standing in conventional postures on either side of the cross.

(vii) Kilchoman No. 53 (XXX *d*) is a fairly plain cross-head with well proportioned Crucifixion.

(viii) Laggan No. 32a (XXXI *a*) is an interesting cross-shaft recently discovered at Laggan in the vicinity of an old chapel by the river. Except for the lower part of a Crucifixion with 'ragged' cross and the roll mouldings at the edges, the obverse is completely blank; what look like remnants of scroll or script are merely breaks in the surface of the stone. This was evidently a disc-headed cross, and a very late one in the series as is plain from the ivy-like foliage on the reverse. Such a style may be seen on slabs in Knapdale, Iona and Oransay of very late 15th or 16th century date.

(ix) Texa No. 105 (XXXI *b*) is part of a cross-shaft originally in that island and now in the National Museum of Antiquities, Edinburgh.* What appears to be the lower part of a Crucifixion on the obverse suggests that it had a disc-head.

The strong probability is that this cross belongs to the second half of the 14th century, the principal clue to dating being the inscription 'HEC EST CRUX REGNALDI JOH(ANN) IS DE YSLA'—'THIS IS THE CROSS OF REGINALD SON OF JOHN OF ISLAY'. There are, it is true, several persons who might conceivably have been called 'Reginald son of John of Islay', but of all the *known* Reginalds the short list of claimants for this stone can be effectively reduced to three.

The first is Reginald, son of John 1st Lord of the Isles by his first marriage with Amie MacRuari heiress of the North Isles. Reginald accepted with a good grace the precedence given to the children of the second marriage with the Lady Margaret, daughter of Robert II. As a vassal of his younger half-brother Donald 2nd Lord, Reginald was the progenitor of Clanranald, the MacDonalds of the North Isles and Garmoran, and he died in 1386.

Secondly, there is Reginald or Ranald, second son of John younger brother of Donald 2nd Lord of the isles. After Donald's accession John was given Dunyveg with 60 Marklands in Islay and 120 in Kintyre, and he acquired the Glens of Antrim by marriage with the heiress. His son Ranald was given some of the Kintyre lands and became the founder of the Clan Ranald-bane of Largie. He must have been dead by about 1480.

Thirdly, there is Reginald, illegitimate son of John 4th Lord of the Isles. There is no reason for attaching much weight to his claim. He is mentioned only once—in 1485 when he witnessed the grant of a charter by his brother Angus, Master of the Isles, in favour of the Abbey of Iona.

Since the island of Texa lies off Dunyveg, Reginald son of John of Dunyveg might seem to be a strong candidate. Other

* For guidance in commenting on this stone I am very specially indebted to Dr Steer. It raises many fascinating problems, but as these can be competently discussed only by the specialist I shall confine myself to indicating the period to which the stone most probably belongs.

considerations, however, tend to weaken his claim. The family possessions in Islay were insignificant in comparison with the lands in Ireland and Kintyre. It is probable that John spent little time in the island, the administration of his part of Islay being apparently committed from about 1408 to a family of MacKays as hereditary 'maors'. Reginald's own lands were in Kintyre, and if he were moved to erect a cross it is unlikely that he would have chosen Texa rather than, say, Killean in Kintyre.

The first mentioned Reginald must, on the other hand, have had a close personal connection with Islay and particularly with the eastern side. He is actually referred to as 'of Islay' in 1372 when Robert II confirms the charter of the North Isles made by 'John of Islay' to 'Reginald of Islay his son'. More significant is the passage in McVurish's history which says that "Ragnall, the son of Eoin, was High Steward over Insigall at the time of his father's death, being in advanced age and ruling over them". Donald, Master of the Isles, can hardly have been more than 20 when his father died in 1380, and during the last few years of the old Lord's life Reginald, as regent, must have been in control of Dunyveg (the principal castle in Islay). This would naturally involve contact with the monastery of Texa. "A man of augmenting churches and monasteries was this Raghnall" says McVurish, and it would have been wholly in character that he should have given a cross to the island.

If it was indeed this Reginald who had the cross erected (it was erected by, not to, him), it must be not later than 1386, the year of his death.

Of the stone's many interesting characteristics two are fairly obvious. First, in the inscription Islay is spelt 'Ysla' (not 'Isla' as Graham read it). The usual spellings of the period were Ila, Ile, Yla, Yle; and with rare exceptions the intrusive 's' does not appear until the 18th century when we get 'Isla'. In the exceptional cases where the 's' occurs in documents of earlier centuries an Anglo-Norman or English influence is operative. Thus the English transcript of Edward Balliol's charter to John of Islay in 1336 has 'Ysle'. One naturally wonders whether the inscription on Reginald's cross has been similarly influenced.

Secondly, there are the decorative motives. On the obverse, the warrior holding an axe is most unusual for Islay. Again, animals are not commonly found on Islay slabs of the 14th century, and the lively group of stag and hounds on the reverse suggests an affinity with Nereabolls No. 71 which, as we saw (p. 35), can hardly be earlier than a 'McEachran' cross-shaft in Kintyre dated to the 15th century.

There are in fact, so many peculiarities about this monument that, while a late 14th century dating is probably correct, its provenance is very puzzling indeed.

(x) Kilarow No. 31 (XXXI *c*) is represented by the lower part of its shaft, though a piece of a sword-slab has been shaped and added to form a tall pillar, the monstrosity now standing in the grounds of Islay House. The scroll-work on the shaft is quite unlike that of the other cross-shafts in the island, resembling more closely that on the Kintyre 'McEachran' shaft (XIX *b*) already mentioned.

The panel shewing a kneeling figure (? woman) with rosary compares with one on an Iona slab (Drummond XXVI, No. 1). Only a few letters of the rather sprawling inscription are legible. Graham thought the name 'PAU(LUS)' to be included, but it looks more like 'PAT . . .'. 'PATRICK' was common in some Islay families, and especially popular with the MacBriuins of Laggan, hereditary chief judges in the island.

(xi) Kilchoman No. 52 (XXXII *a*) is a good head with a considerable section of the shaft.

(xii) Kilchoman No. 47 (XXXII *b*) is a beautiful shaft. On the obverse, the upper part of the fragment shews that the Crucifixion with 'ragged' cross had occupied the head and part of the shaft; and the figure of an ecclesiastic is also discernible.

(xiii) Nereabolls Nos. 62 and 63 (XXXIII) are two pieces constituting the head and part of the shaft of an interesting stone. The outline of the cross-head leaves much to be desired, but the decoration on the reverse is good. Presumably the canopied figure on the obverse of the shaft represents the prior of a local monastery (the staff turned outward does not, as is sometimes stated, necessarily represent a bishop rather than an abbot). The name 'ODON . .' discernible in the inscription, standing for the Latin form of 'Aodh', suggests that the ecclesiastic concerned may have been one of the MacKays of the Rhinns. In March 1428 Angus, Bishop of Sodor (he was a younger brother of Donald, 2nd Lord of the Isles), accepted responsibility for payment of the annates of the parish church of Kilchoman in Islay (Yle) void by the death of Odo Macayg (Aodh MacAoidh—Hugh MacKay or Magee or MacCuaig).

(xiv) Kilchoman No. 50 (xxxiv) shews two parts of a cross, now re-united and housed in the Museum. The inscription has been deciphered as 'HEC EST CRUX FAC(TA) PRO ANIMABUS DONCANI MECINNIRLEGIN ET MARI ET MICHAELIS'—'THIS IS A CROSS MADE FOR THE SOULS OF DUNCAN MACINNIRLEGIN AND MARY AND MICHAEL'. Curious as the wording may seem, 'Mary' and 'Michael' must refer to the Virgin and to the Archangel who frequently appears on these crosses as slaying the dragon. The name 'MacInnirlegin' is explained by Professor W. J. Watson as 'son of the lector' (*fear leighinn*), the head of the monastic school. From evidence in the papal registers referring to a connection of 'Macinnerlegyns' with Kilchoman, Watson thinks this cross could be dated to about 1450.

(xv) Kilchoman No. 39 (xxxv), the second of the two unbroken mediaeval crosses in Islay, is now known as 'The Kilchoman Cross'. It stands 8 ft. 4 in. high in the churchyard and is described in detail by Graham whose excellent photographs are now more easily followed than the lichen-covered designs on the stone itself. It belongs to the finest group of mediaeval crosses in the West Highlands and Isles. Most of them are disc-headed with slightly projecting arms, though the Inveraray Cross, despite its unusual head, is of the same family.

From our illustrations it will be obvious that the great majority of the Islay mediaeval crosses belonged to this class, the one under discussion being the most elaborate and finely finished of them all.

On the obverse, the head is dominated by the Crucifixion. On either side of the central Figure are the Virgin Mary and St John, with attendant angels in the background. Below, at the top of the shaft, are two clerics under a double canopy.

Next we have an inscription of fourteen lines which has been partially read by Graham:

'HEC EST C/RUX ..../..E........./.TRIC......./
DI....PRO A/NIMA SUI PAT/RIS ET UXORI/S SUE AC OMN/
IUM FIDELIUM/DE FUNCTOR/.ET..DICTI../......T...../
............/............'

Though there are many gaps in the reading, we can at least understand that someone (called Patrick?) caused the cross to be made for the soul of his father and of his own wife together with those of all faithful departed. Then follow, in descending order, a panel of foliage, a horseman, and finally a panel of interlace—the whole included within a triple-moulding border.

On the reverse, the head is covered with most intricate interlace, and the shaft has five 'rings' of beautifully executed foliage. The first two are formed by intertwining stems rising from the tails of paired beasts; and then, by an ingeniously smooth transition, one of the stems continues as three 'rings' of single-stem serpentine.

The dating of this cross is controversial. While there may be an appreciable gap between it and, say, the MacLean Cross in Iona, it is almost certainly contemporary with the high crosses of Campbeltown and Oransay. This, according to a widely held view, ought to fix its date with fair precision since the inscription on the Campbeltown Cross has been supposed to indicate a date about 1500, and that on the Oransay Cross one of approximately 1510. On the other hand, these inferences from the inscriptions have been challenged. The Campbeltown dating depends on some rather speculative identification of the persons and places referred to; and there are two different readings of the Oransay inscription. One reading is 'HEC EST CRUX COLINI PRIOR ORISOI OBIT MDX . . .' —'THIS IS THE CROSS OF COLIN PRIOR OF ORANSAY DIED 151 . . .'. The other is 'HEC EST CRUX COLINI FILII CRISTI . . .'—'THIS IS THE CROSS OF COLIN SON OF CRISTI(NUS?) . . .'. Loder, in his volume *Colonsay and Oronsay*, supports the first reading in attributing the memorial to Prior Colin. Dr Steer does not.

Nevertheless, there is a line of argument, independent of these inscriptions, relevant to the Kilchoman Cross at least. If we are right in holding that the finest 'ring' form of single-stem serpentine on the Islay slabs belongs to the second half of the 15th century (see above, pp. 32-33), this should determine the period of the Kilchoman Cross; and it is difficult to resist the view that the Kilchoman, Campbeltown and Oransay Crosses are, broadly speaking, contemporary.

(3) *General Remarks on the Mediaeval Crosses*

Their Condition

It is remarkable that the great majority of our mediaeval crosses are broken. We have shafts minus heads, and heads minus shafts. In some cases at least the damage must have been deliberate, but the history of Islay during the early Reformation period does not favour the view that the iconoclasts were of the local population. Suspicion for at least some of the damage attaches most strongly to a certain Archibald Campbell, bailie of Kintyre, who took a prominent part in the final expulsion of the MacDonalds in 1615 and claims to have burned a lot of images he found in the island. What gave most offence was apparently the representation of the Crucifixion, and one wonders how the Kilchoman Cross escaped the fate of its kind. It is noteworthy that in the very citadels of Presbyterianism in Argyll gentler methods were employed to discourage idolatry. Both at Inveraray and at Campbeltown the offending figures were carefully erased, leaving blank panels; otherwise the crosses were preserved undamaged. But such methods were presumably too dilatory and latitudinarian for the Elijahs dedicated to the enlightenment of Islay.

Their Place of Origin

It is often asserted of the West Highland crosses and slabs that they were 'taken from Iona'. As it stands, this statement is so sweeping that it cannot be usefully discussed. In considering how far it is likely to be true of any particular specimen or group it will be useful to distinguish two different questions: *First*, of what material are the monuments made? and *Second*, is the character and quality of the workmanship such as to suggest Iona as the most likely place of its performance? Thus, in the case of the High Cross of Kildalton, the character and quality of the work at once point to Iona, but we know the cross must have been made at Kildalton itself. It is made of local bluestone, and it would have been silly to transport the huge block to Iona with all the dangers involved in bringing back the finished monument. Common sense would dictate bringing the masons to Islay. On the other hand some of the finest cross-slabs, such as the little long-cross one at Finlaggan, might have been made in Iona, and so special interest will attach to the actual provenance of the material. But of course, source of materials is by no means conclusive as to where the work was done. Thus the petrological report furnished to Mr Stevenson on the St John's Cross in Iona indicated that the stone must have been quarried in the Kilmartin-Knapdale area; but no one seriously suggests that it was carved on the mainland. The presumption is that the pieces of which it is constructed (see p. 16) were imported in a rough-hewn state.

So far as the mediaeval disc-headed crosses are concerned, I think the question of an Iona origin can be settled without much discussion of the locality from which the material was taken. These crosses exhibit a considerable variety, from the MacMillan's in Knapdale to the High Cross of Oransay, but we shall restrict our consideration to those of Kilchoman, Campbeltown and Oransay.

We can agree that all the constituent elements in the decoration are found on Iona slabs. But the combination of these with a more or less elaborate representation of the Crucifixion on a disc-headed cross is another matter. There is only one certain example of the kind in Iona, namely the MacLean Cross. The MacKinnon Cross of 1489 was *probably* disc-headed. Perhaps the 60 (or was it 365?) thrown into the sea by the puritans were all disc-headed, but these are even more shy of rediscovery than the Tobermory treasure; and probable or hypothetical examples are not evidence. The only real evidence is the MacLean Cross, and this is surely not to be regarded as a model or progenitor of the Oransay-Campbeltown-Kilchoman group, but only as an imitation. Its 'foliage' does not have the coherent pattern of the main group, and even the panel of simple interlace matting has not been regularly laid out. In short, Iona does not seem to have been intimately concerned in the development of this kind of monument, and the most plausible guess, perhaps, is that the best examples are the work of a select school based on Oransay. At the same time, in view of the high concentration of disc-headed crosses in the Rhinns of Islay, it may be inferred that there was in this area a local sculptor's yard. If so it may sometime be discovered by the archaeologists.

NOTE. These pages were passed for press before Dr Steer's most illuminating Rhind Lectures on 'Late Mediaeval Monumental Sculpture in the West Highlands'. Important points relevant to the Islay stones are the following: though our slabs are predominantly of the Iona School, some are associated with Knapdale and Kintyre, and at least one (No. 101, xxv *b*) is of Colonsay origin; the quarries for West Highland stones have been mainly (though not exclusively) in the Loch Awe-Knapdale area; and Dr Steer gives our disc-headed crosses a much closer Iona connection than is suggested on this concluding page.

GRAHAM'S INDEX OF ISLAY CARVED STONES

(With Additions in Brackets)

Keills

1. Slab: galley, paired beasts, foliage, sword; later inscription 'D M E 1707'.
2. Cross-shaft.

Finlaggan

3. Slab: warrior, inscription.
4. Slab: 3 swords, crosses.
5. Slab: anvil, scroll.
6. Slab: unfinished fragment.
7. Slab: foliage, sword.
8. Slab: long-cross, foliage, sword.
9. Slab: fragments, cross.
10. Slab: long-cross, foliage, sword.
11. Slab: plain, triple-moulding.
12. Slab—part: rope-moulding.

(12a. Stone with interlacing-band cross; found Balulive.)

Kilmeny

13. Slab: panel, paired beasts, foliage.
14. Slab: top worn, good foliage.
15. Slab: sword, dragon.

Kilarow

16. Slab: upper part altered and dated, Fraser inscription on borders.
17. Slab: inscription, chalice, priest, cross-head, foliage.
18. Slab: warrior.
19. Slab: broken, sword, carving.
20. Slab: foliage, mythical animals, late sword.
21. Slab: broken, warrior.
22. Slab: cross-head, animals, defaced by later inscription.
23. Slab: cross-head, foliage, sword.
24. Slab: cross-head, priest, chalice, foliage.
25. Slab: border, top interlace, foliage, sword.
26. Slab: interlace panel, figure in niche, shears.
27. Slab: scroll, sword.
28. Cross-head fragment.
29. Slab: long-cross, foliage, sword.
30. Slab: cross-head, mythical animals, foliage, late sword.
31. Cross-shaft with alien addition: scroll, animals, woman with rosary, horseman, inscription.
32. Decorated plinth of 31.

(*Laggan*

32a. Cross-shaft: late foliage.

32b. Cross-slab: incised, with two rings.)

Kilnave

33. Kilnave High Cross.
34. Slab: foliage, sword, animals, inscription.

(34a. Slab: thin, shaped, pierced, inside church.)

Kilchoman

35. Slab: priest in niche.
36. Slab: priest.
37. Slab: faint scroll.
38. Slab: traces of sword.
39. 'The Kilchoman Cross'.
40. Slab: cross-head, foliage, sword, Campbell additions 1678.

41. Slab: cross-head, foliage, sword.
42. Slab: cross-head, scroll, sword, Campbell inscription 1663.
43. Slab: worn, cross-head, sword.
44. Slab: worn, scroll, sword, animals, galley (later?) upside down.
45. Slab: sword, galley (possibly late copy), 1618 Campbell inscription.
46. Slab: trace of sword.
47. Cross-shaft, scroll, figures.
48. Slab: large sword.
49. Slab: priest, 18th century McLachlan inscription.
50. 'MacInnirlegin Cross'.
51. Slab: scroll, sword, later McLachlan inscription.
52. Cross-head: obverse Crucifixion, reverse foliage.
53. Cross-head: Crucifixion.
54. 'Sanctuary cross', NE of church.
55. 'Sanctuary cross', S of church.

Kilchiaran

56. Slab: traces of sword.
57. Slab: priest in niche, cross-head.
58. Font.
59. Slab: cross-head, foliage, sword.
60. Slab: cross-head, foliage, sword.
61. Cupped stone.

Nereabolls

62 & 63. Head and shaft of cross: Crucifixion, priest in niche, foliage.
64. Slab: traces of carving.
65. Slab: cross-head, foliage, sword.
66. Font or basin.
67. Slab: fragment of, with 'marigold' (?)
68. Slab: faint scroll and sword.
69. Slab: cross-head, chalice, priest, animals, foliage.
70. Slab: 'Vine and Branches'.
71. Slab: galley, interlace, foliage, sword, animals.
72. Slab: broken, cross-head, foliage, sword, animals.
73. Slab: cross-head, foliage, sword.

(*Gleann na Gaoithe*

73a. Roughly shaped cross.
73b. Slab: incised outline Celtic-ring cross.
73c. Slab: Celtic-ring cross in semi-relief, crosslets.

Eilean Orsay

73d. Slab: fragments, incised outline ring cross, crosslets.)

Kilnaughton

74. Slab: warrior, small figure, shears.
75. Slab: cross-head, foliage, sword.
76. Slab: small cross, shears, foliage.
(76a. Slab: exposed and reburied, 1963)

Port Ellen Area

77. Slab: Kilbride, ring cross in relief.
78. Cup stone.
107. Slab: 'Doid Mhairi' stone.

Kildalton

79. Kildalton High Cross.
(79a. Slab: incised outline cross.)
80. Mediaeval cross.
81. Slab: fragments, hunter, horn, hounds.
82. Slab: fragments, faint carving.
83. Font or basin.
84. Slab: fragment, cross-head.
85. Piscina.
86. Slab: warrior, inscription, small figure, dog.

87. Slab: pattern weathered away.
88. Slab: primitive, cross in relief.
89. Slab: long-cross, foliage, sword.
90. Slab: warrior in low relief, MacIan inscription.
91. Slab: saltire-&-ring, foliage, sword.
92. Slab: fragment, stag and hounds.
93. Slab: gun, etc., McArthor 1696.
94. Slab: fragment of ring-cross slab.
95. Slab: poor, later 'Hew McLeod 1716'.
96. Slab: incised rapier, 'James Steward'.
97. Slab: traces of sculpture.
98. Slab: saltire-&-ring, sword, interlace, fish and otter.
99. Slab: long-cross, foliage, sword.
100. Slab: saltire-&-ring, sword, unusual foliage and figures, shears.
101. Slab: two figures under canopy, cross-head, galley, border inscription.

Texa

102. Slab: part, priest, border inscription.
103. & 104. Figures from broken cross-head used as plinth for 105.
105. Cross-shaft of 'Reginald', figures, inscription.
106. Slab: design faint, sword, two figures meeting.
[107. See 'Port Ellen Area'.]

('*Islay*'

108. Cross-head: fragment, cross-crosslet of interwoven bands.
109. Cross-head: fragment of 'disc head', part of Crucifixion.)

GRAHAM'S CHARTS OF THE PRINCIPAL STONES

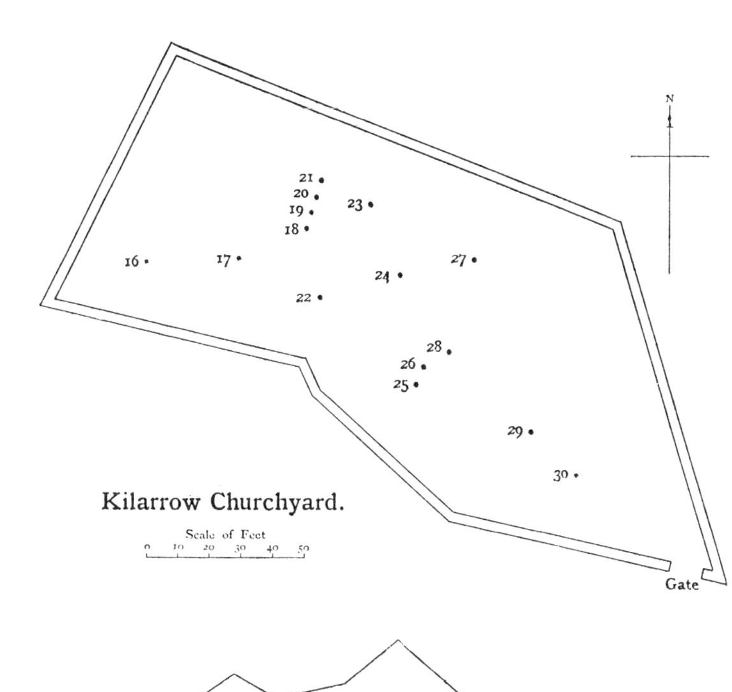

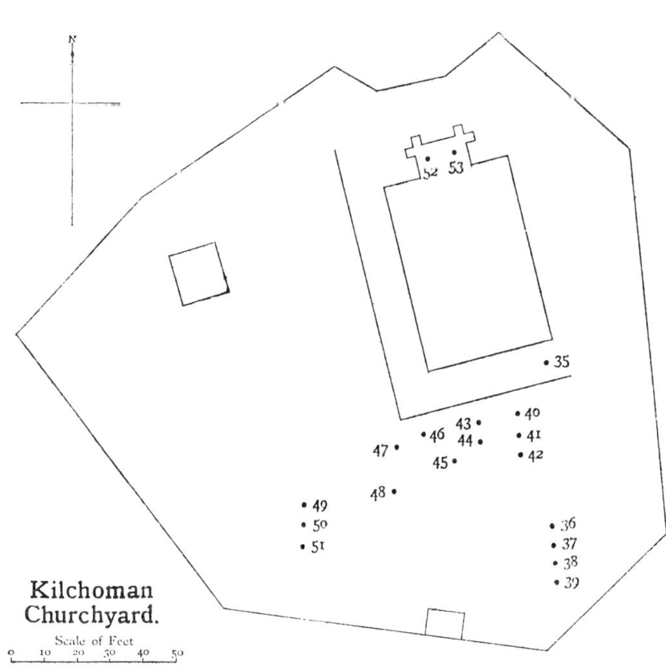

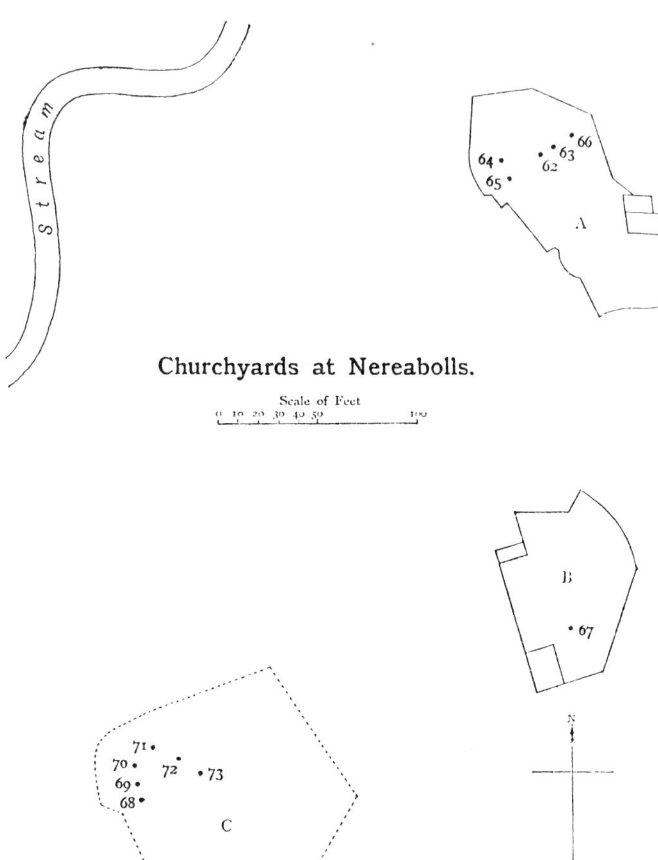

Churchyards at Nereabolls.

80

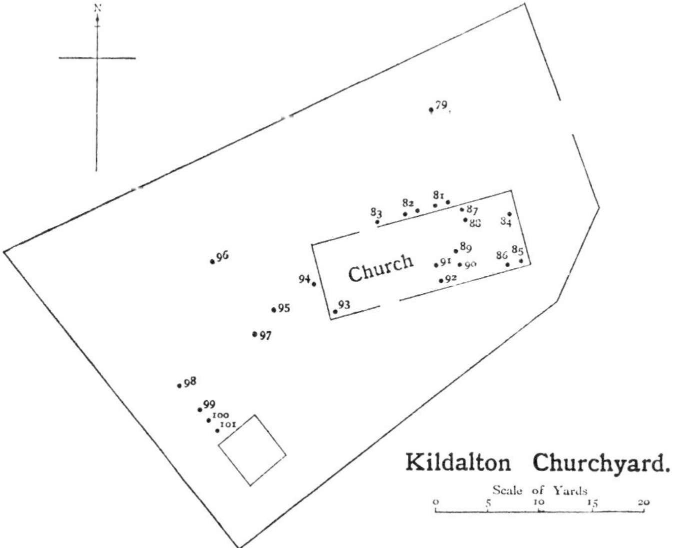
N
79
83
82
81
87
88
84
Church
89
91
90
86
85
92
94
93
96
95
97
98
99
100
101
Kildalton Churchyard.
Scale of Yards
0 5 10 15 20

PRINCIPAL PLACE-NAMES

Grid References to the One-inch Ordnance Survey Maps

NR328478	Carragh Bhan.
403695	Cil Eileagain (Balulive)
299669	Cil Eileagain (Craigens).
356459	'Doid Mhairi'.
406455	Dunyveg.
164517	Eilean Orsay.
388681	Finlaggan.
212536	Gleann na Gaoithe.
336628	Islay House.
414686	Keills { Chapel.
417687	Keills { Cross-shaft.
336626	Kilarow.
385465	Kilbride.
205601	Kilchiaran.
216632	Kilchoman.
458508	Kildalton.
388653	Kilmeny
345453	Kilnaughton.
286715	Kilnave.
422673	Kilslevan.
320484	Kintra.
295559	Laggan chapel site (much eroded).
292759	Nave Island.
226550	Nereabolls.
391438	Texa.
299474	Tokamol.

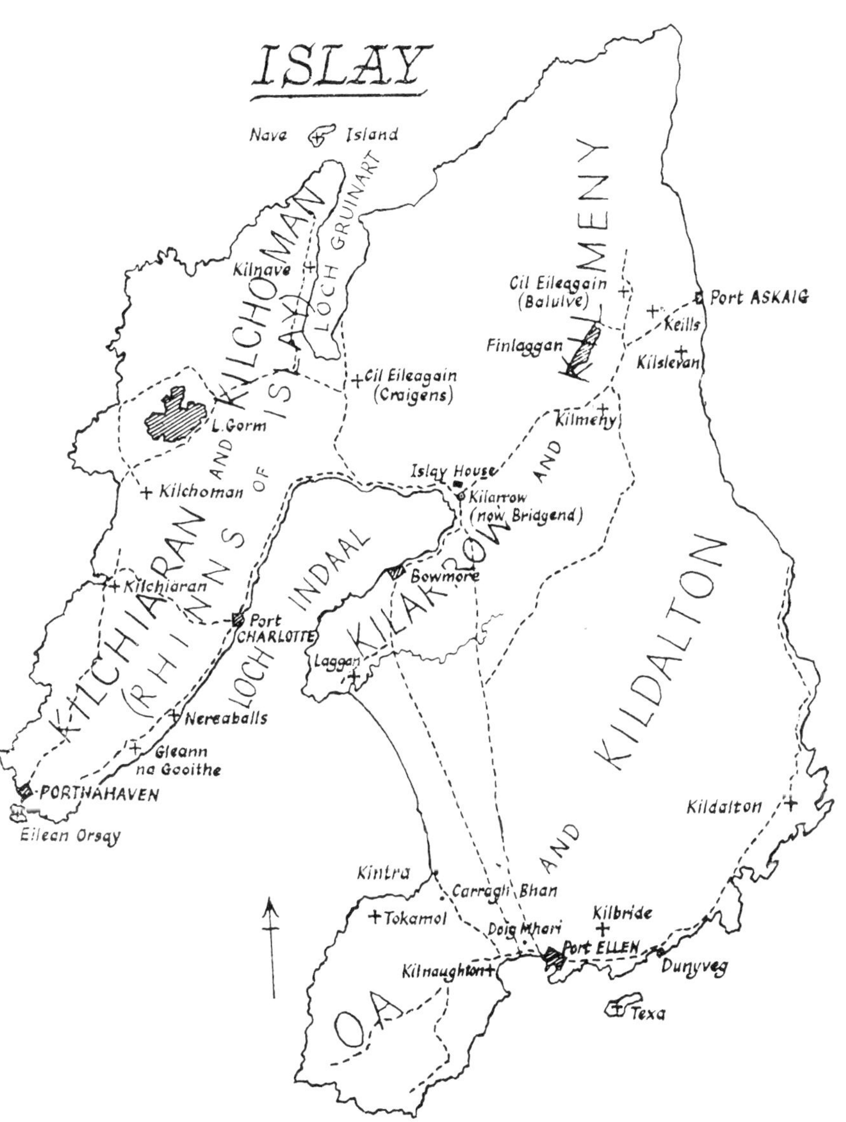
ISLAY
Nave Island
LOCH GRUINART
KILCHOMAN
KILMENY
Kilnave
Cil Eileagain
(Baluive)
Port ASKAIG
Keills
Finlaggan
Kilslevan
Cil Eileagain
(Craigens)
L. Gorm
ISLAY
OF
AND
Kilmeny
Islay House
Kilarrow
(now Bridgend)
Kilchoman
RHINNS
KILCHIARAN
LOCH INDAAL
KILARROW
AND
Bowmore
KILDALTON
Kilchiaran
Port
CHARLOTTE
Laggan
LOCH
Nereaballs
Gleann
na Gooithe
PORTNAHAVEN
Eilean Orsay
Kildalton
AND
Kintra
Carragh Bhan
Tokamol
Doig Mhairi
Kilbride
Port ELLEN
Dunyveg
Kilnaughton
OA
Texa

BIBLIOGRAPHY

GRAHAM, R. C., *The Carved Stones of Islay* (1895).

ALLEN, J. ROMILLY (and ANDERSON, J.), *The Early Christian Monuments of Scotland* (1903).

ASHDOWN, C. H., *British and Foreign Arms and Armour* (1909).

COLLINGWOOD, W. G., *Northumbrian Crosses of the Pre-Norman Age* (1927).

CURLE (Mrs), CECIL L., "The Chronology of the Early Christian Monuments of Scotland" in *Proc. Soc. Antiq. Scot.*, LXXIV (1939-40).

CUTTS, E. L., *Manual of Sepulchral Slabs and Crosses* (1849).

DRUMMOND, J., *Sculptured Monuments of Iona and the West Highlands* (1881).

GRAHAM, H. D., *Antiquities of Iona* (1880).

GRANT, I. F., *The Lordship of the Isles* (1935).

HENRY, F., *La Sculpture Irlandaise* (1933).

— *Irish High Crosses* (1964).

— "Early Monasteries, etc." in *Proc. Royal Irish Acad.*, 58, Sect. C.

— *L'Art Irlandais* (3 vols., 1963-4).

KENDRICK, T. D., *Anglo-Saxon Art to A.D.* 900 (1938).

— *Late Saxon and Viking Art* (1949).

KERMODE, P. M. C., *Manx Crosses* (1907).

LAMONT, W. D., *The Early History of Islay* (1966).

LIONARD, P., "Early Irish Grave Slabs" in *Proc. Royal Irish Acad.*, 61, Sect. C.

LODER, J. DE V., *Colonsay and Oronsay* (1935).

NASH-WILLIAMS, V. E., *Early Christian Monuments of Wales* (1950).

DE PAOR, M. and L., *Early Christian Ireland* (1958).

Proceedings of the Society of Antiquaries of Scotland (consult Indices under 'Crosses', 'Slabs', 'Islay', etc.).

RADFORD, C. A. RALEGH, "The Early Christian Monuments of Scotland" in *Antiquity*, XVI, No. 61 (March 1942).

ROE, HELEN M., "The Irish High Cross: Morphology and Iconography" in *Journal of Royal Soc. Antiq. Ireland*, Vol. 95 (1965).

STEVENSON, R. B. K., "Chronology and Relationship of Some Irish and Scottish Crosses" in *Journal of Royal Soc. Antiq. Ireland*, LXXXVI, Part I (1956).

STUART, J., *Sculptured Stones of Scotland* (2 vols. 1856-67).

WHITE, T. P., *Archaeological Sketches in Scotland: Kintyre* (1873).

Archaeological Sketches in Scotland: Knapdale and Gigha (1875).

PLATE I

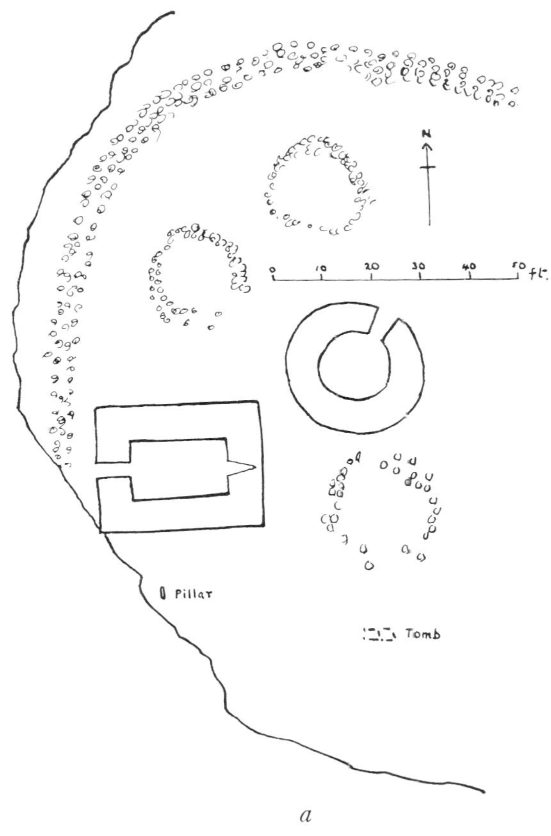

a

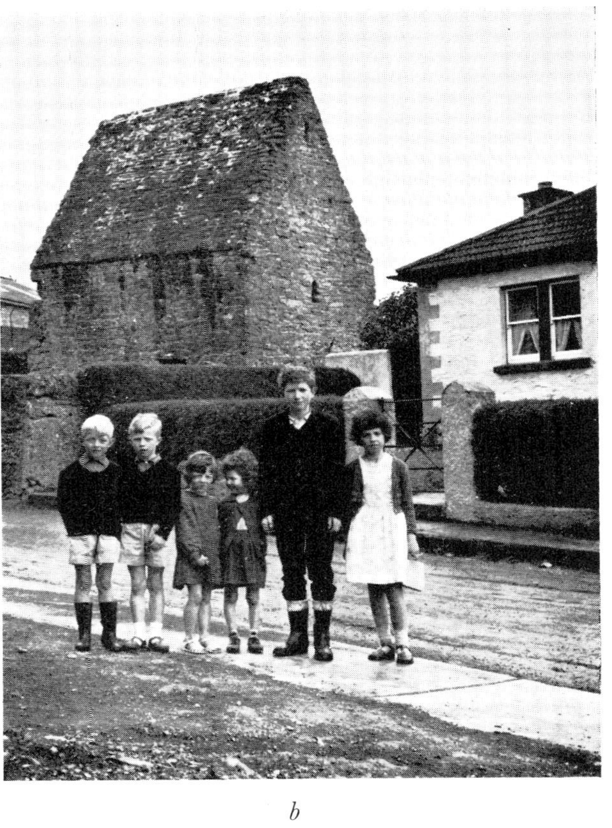

b

PLATE II

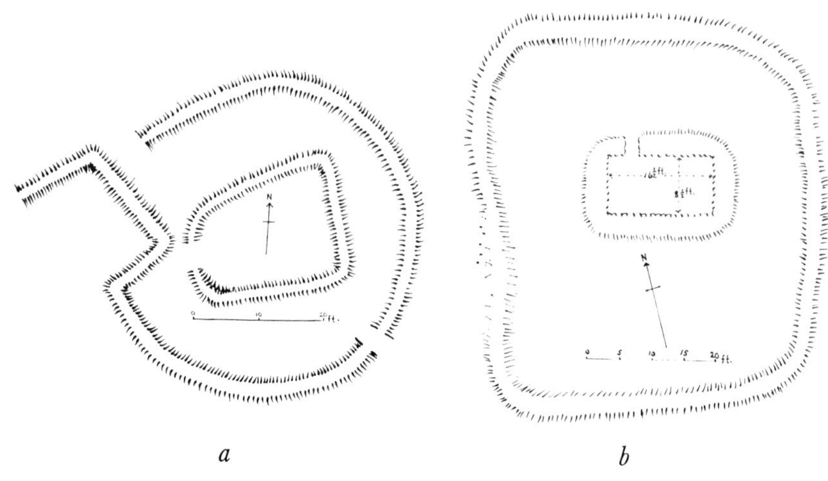

a *b*

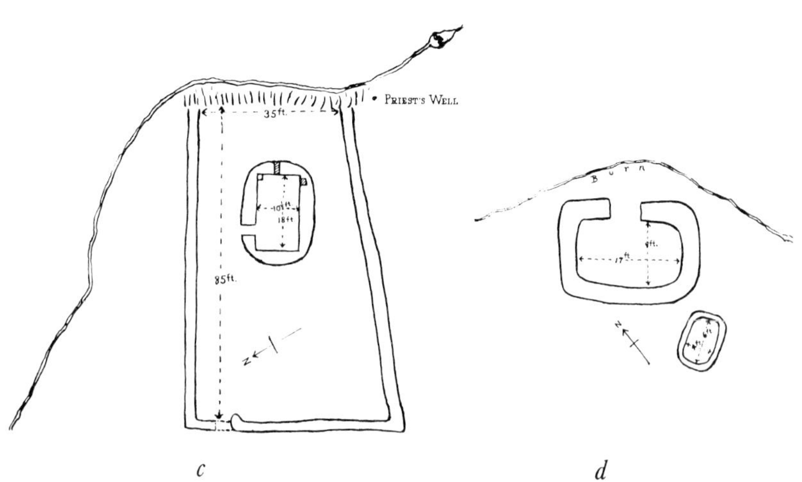

c *d*

a

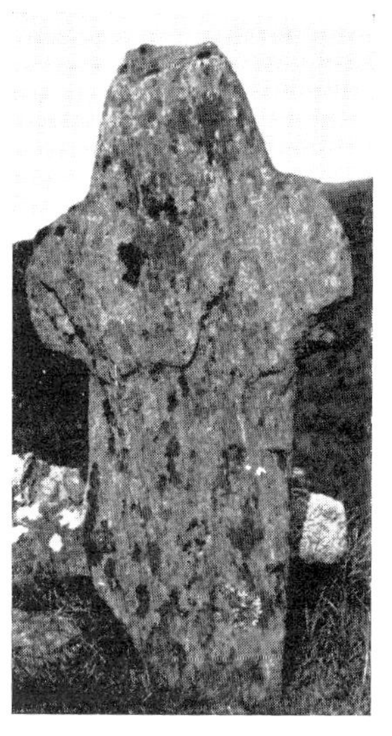

c

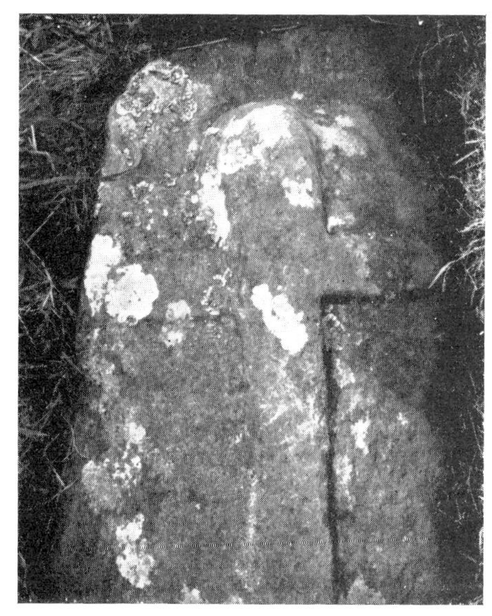

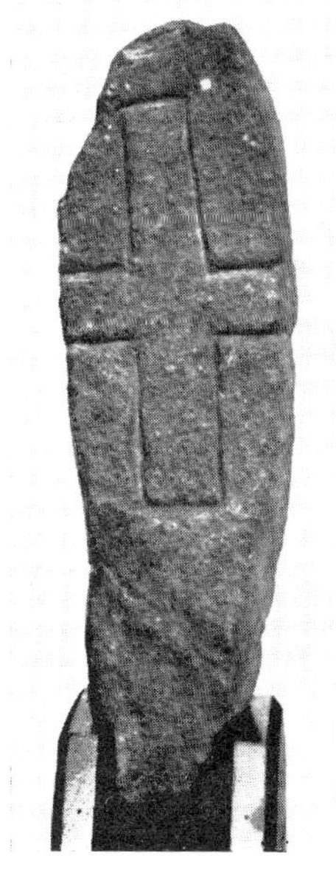

b

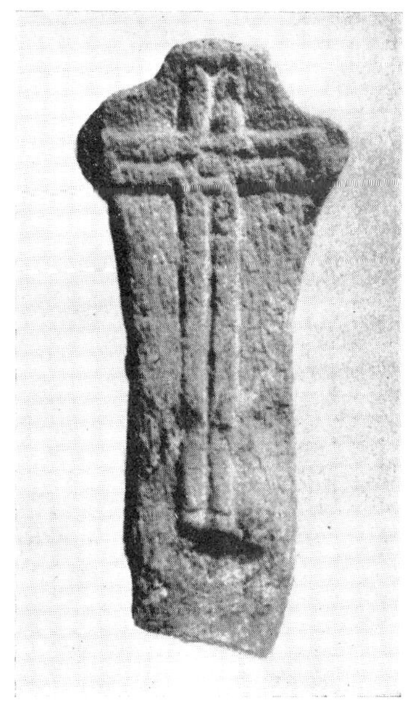

d

Plate IV

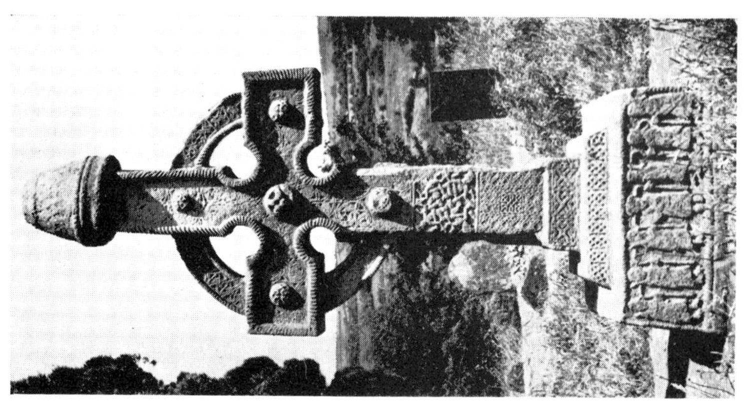

c

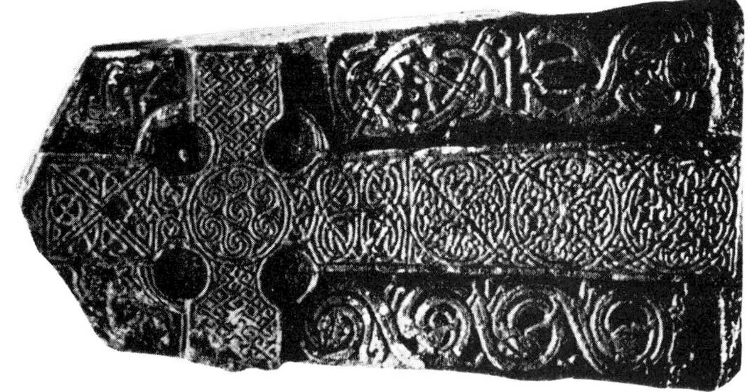

b

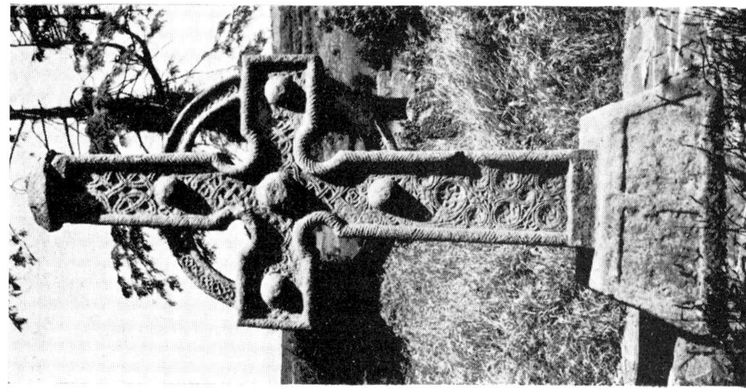

a

PLATE V

a

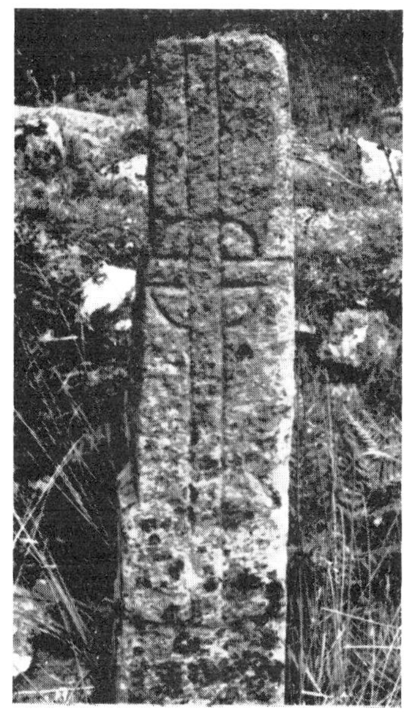

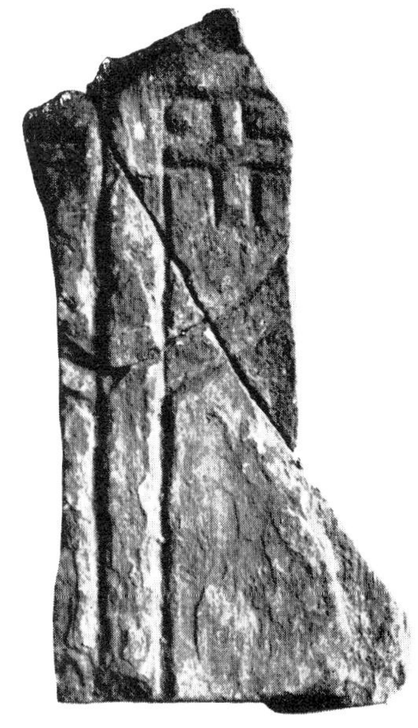

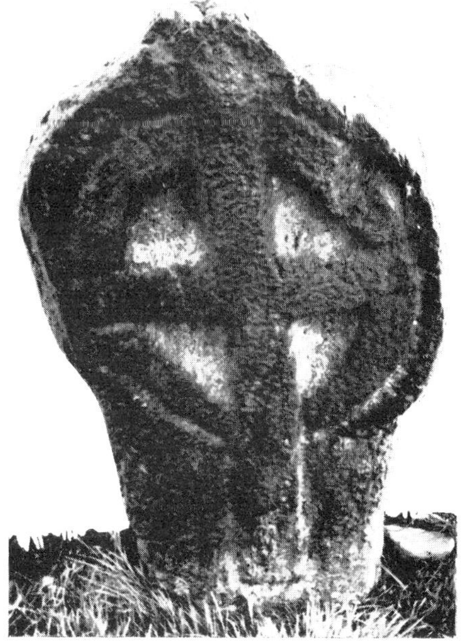

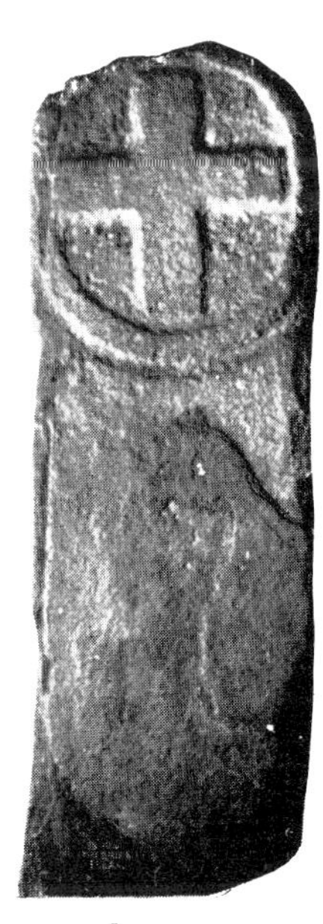

c

d

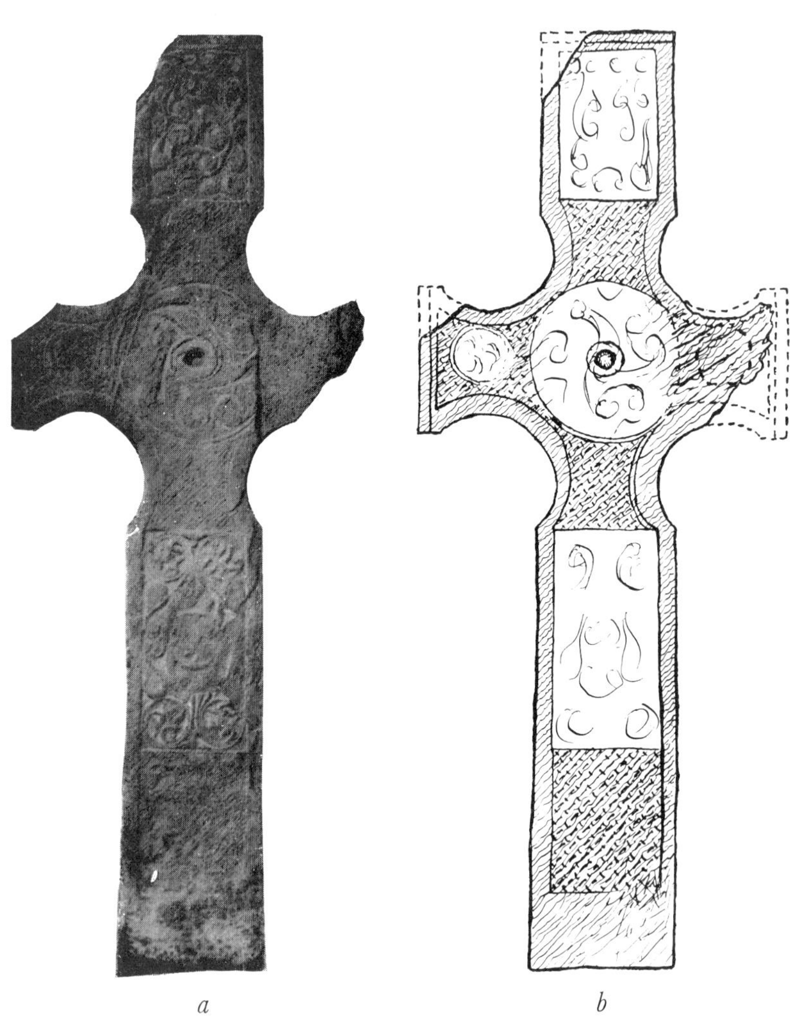

a *b*

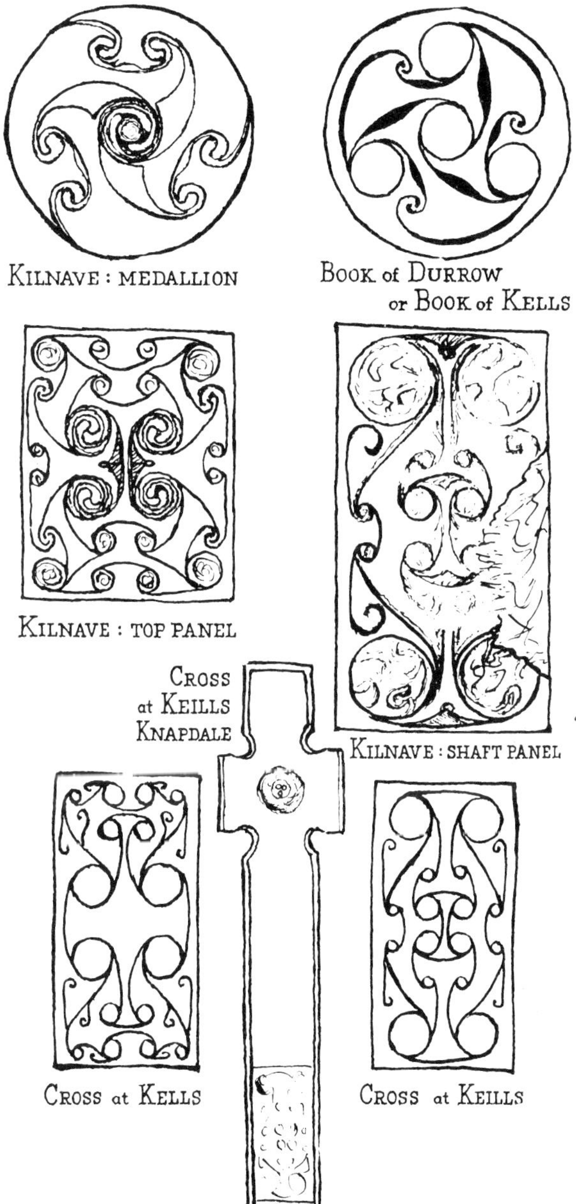
KILNAVE : MEDALLION
BOOK of DURROW
or BOOK of KELLS
KILNAVE : TOP PANEL
KILNAVE : SHAFT PANEL
CROSS
at KEILLS
KNAPDALE
CROSS at KELLS
CROSS at KEILLS

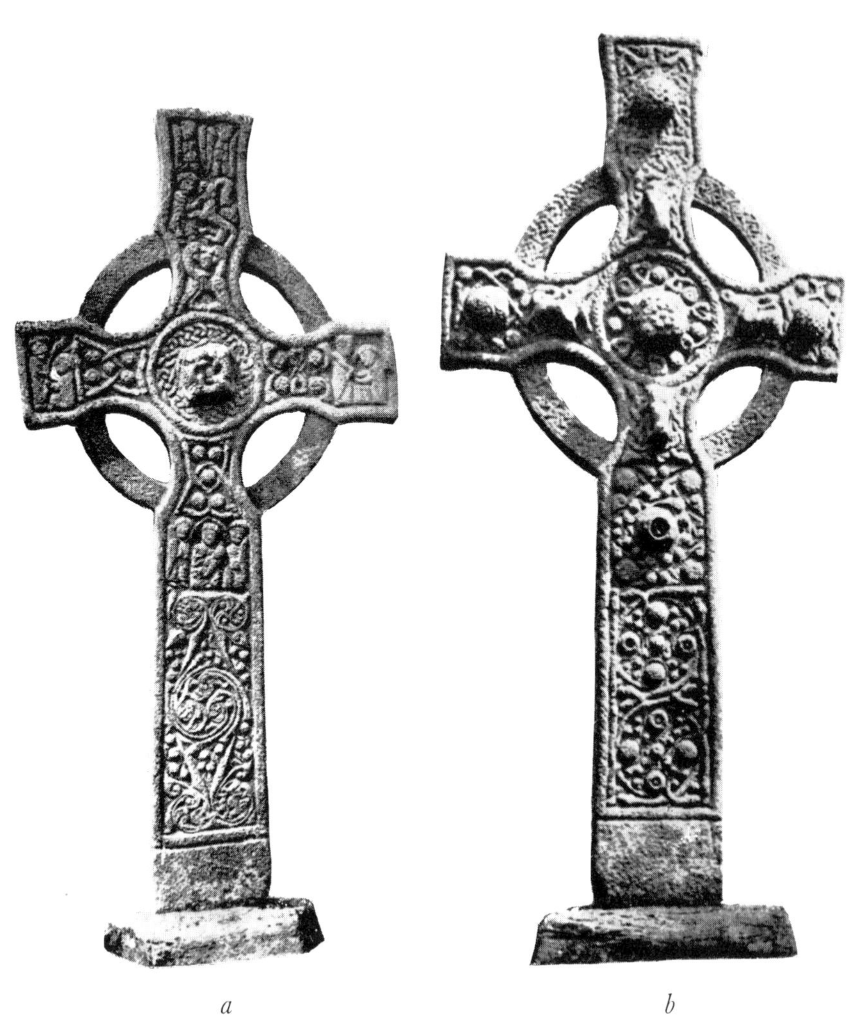

a *b*

a *b*

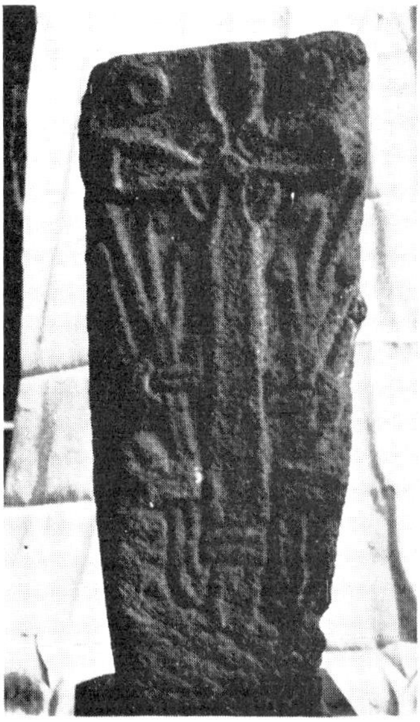

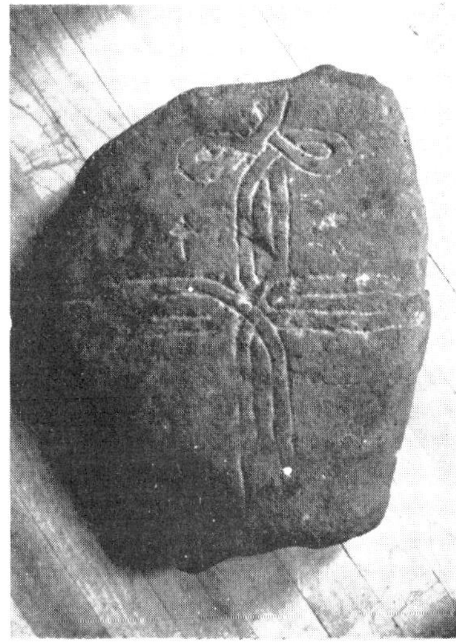

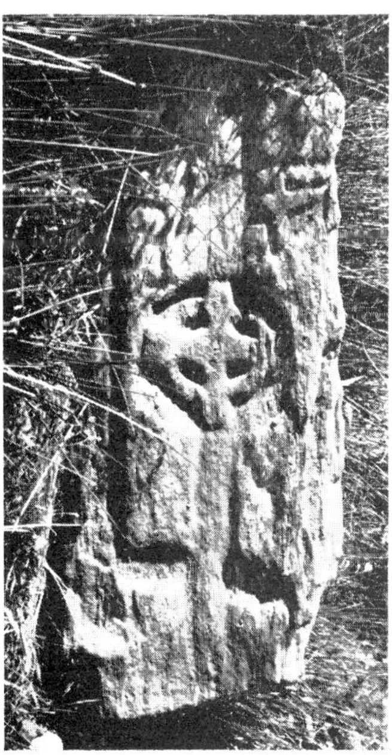

c 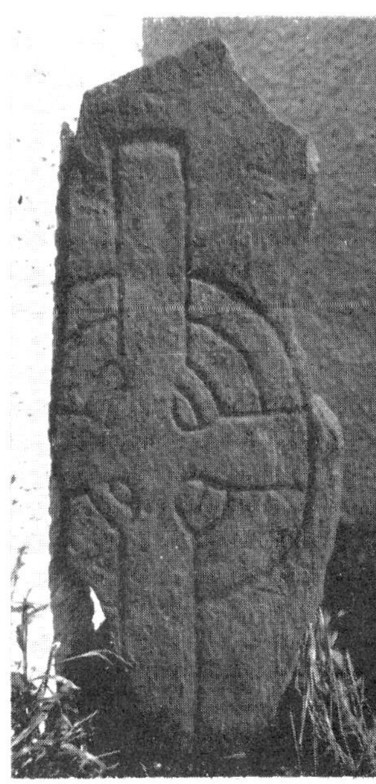 *d*

PLATE X

a

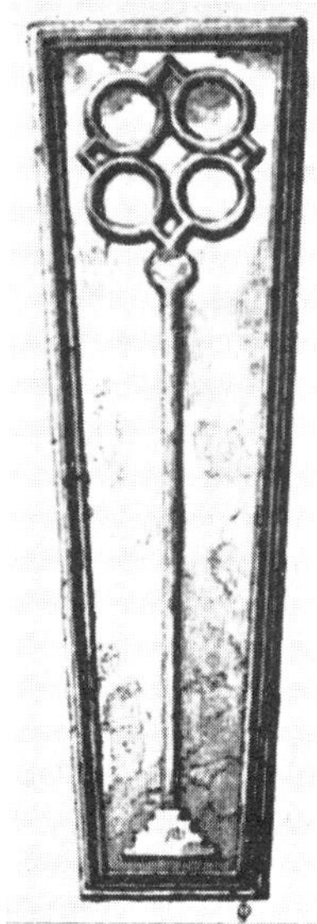

b

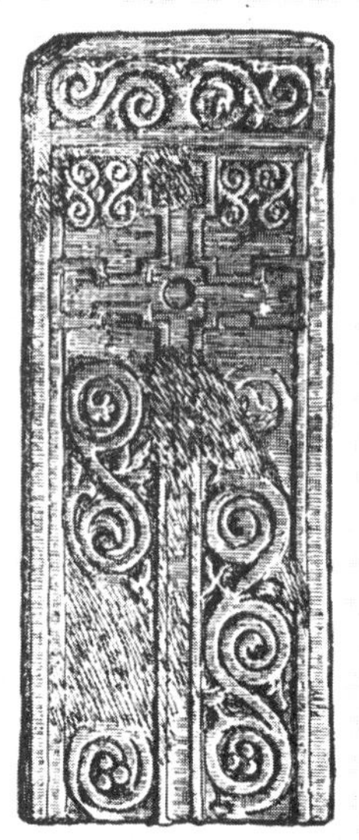

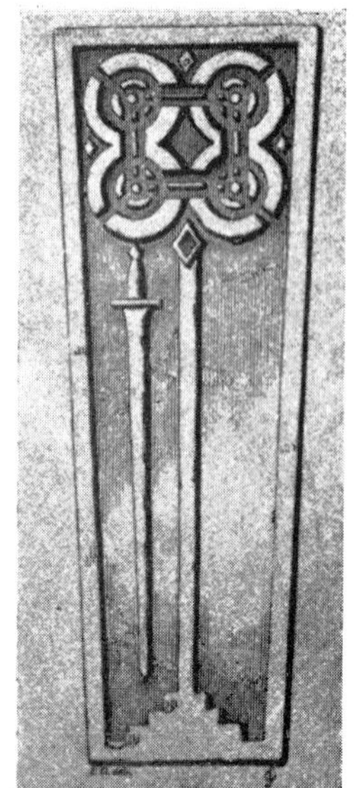

c

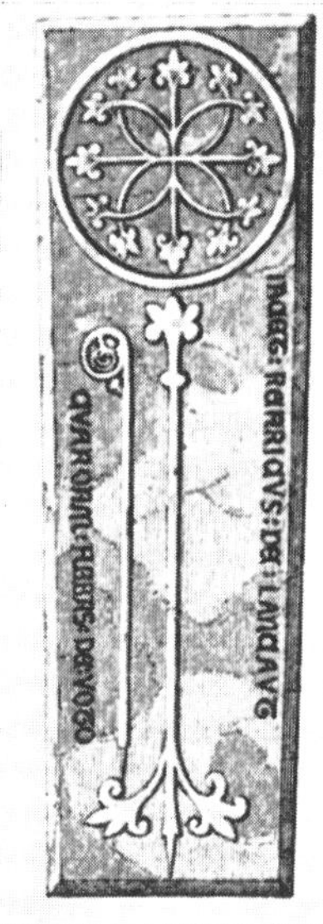

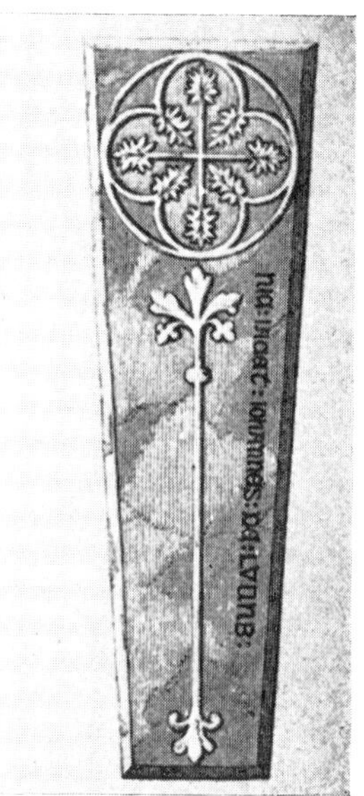

d

PLATE XI

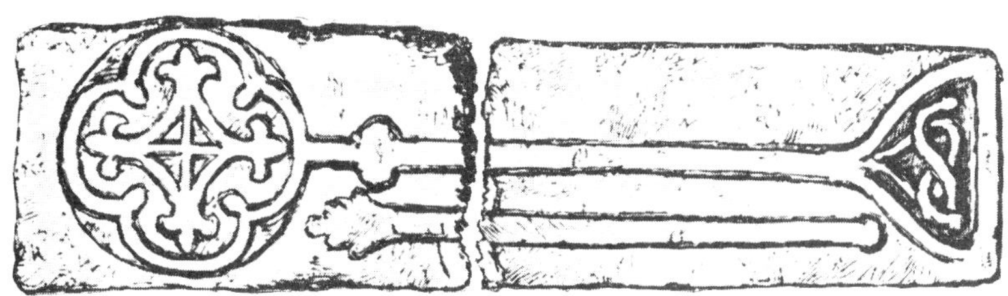

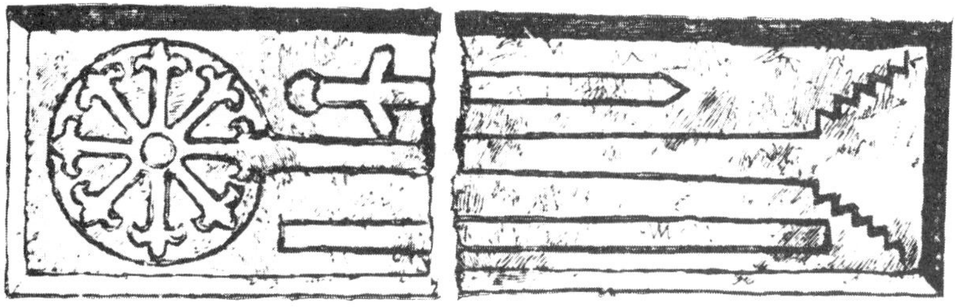

b

a

PLATE XII

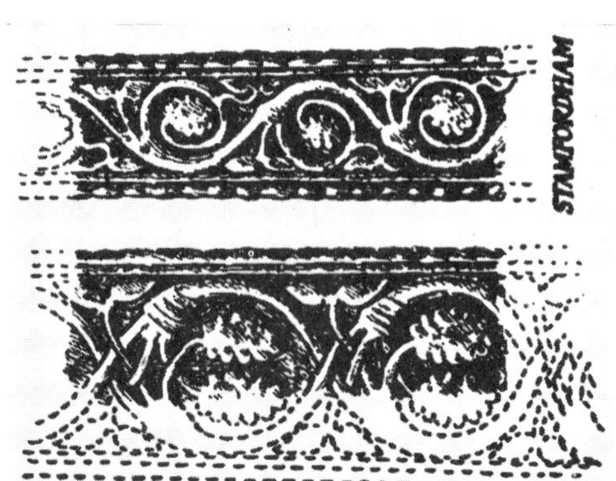

c

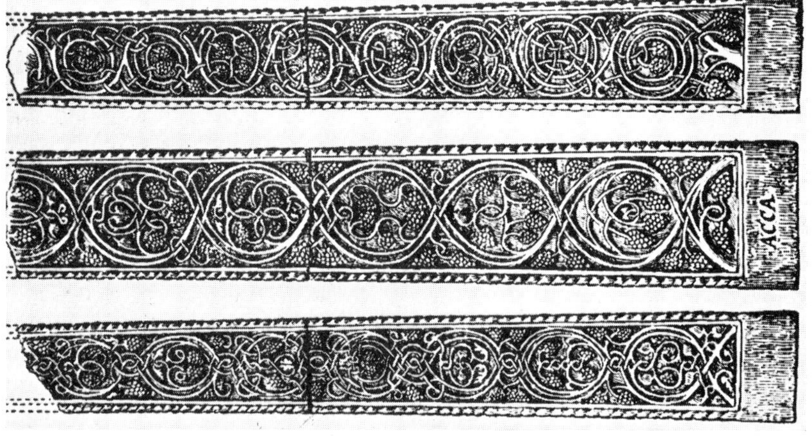

a

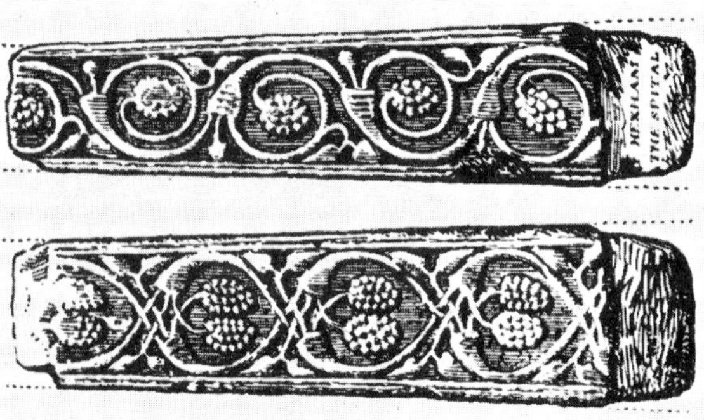

b

PLATE XIII

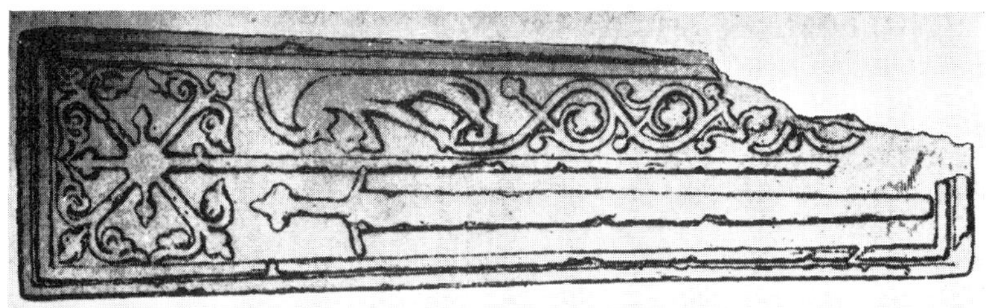

d

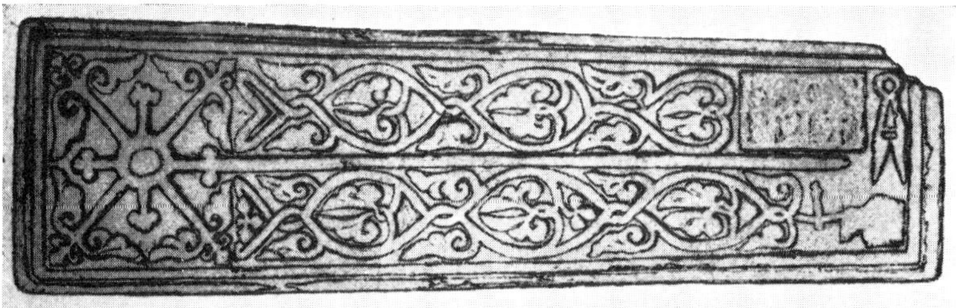

c

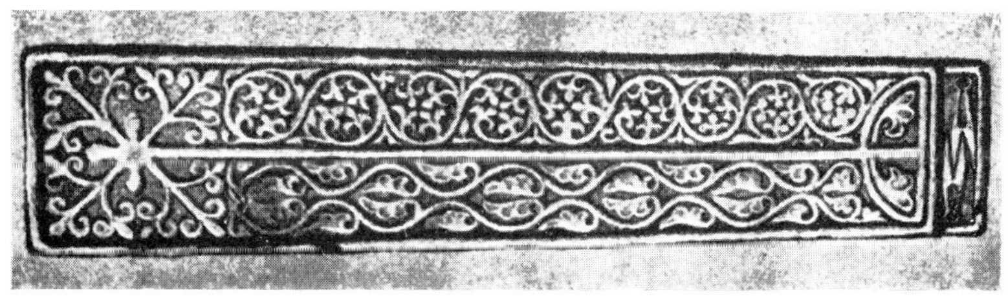

b

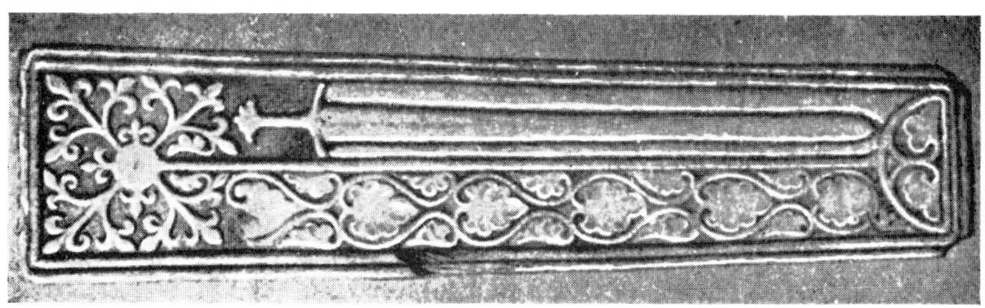

a

PLATE XIV

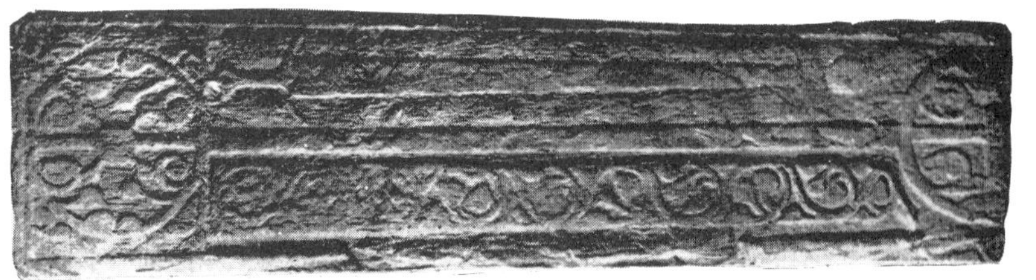
c

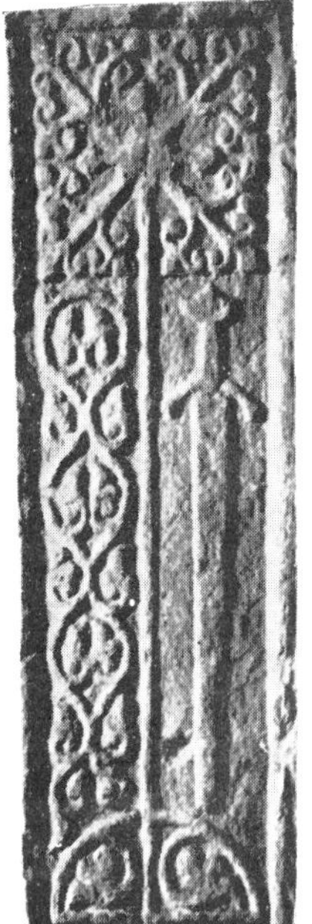
a

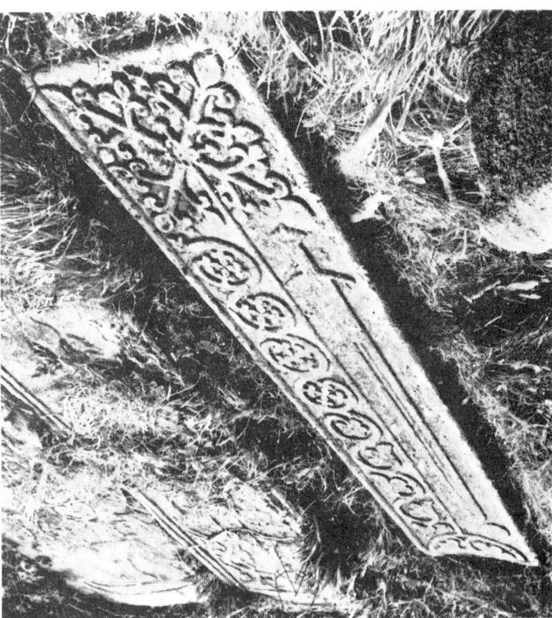
d

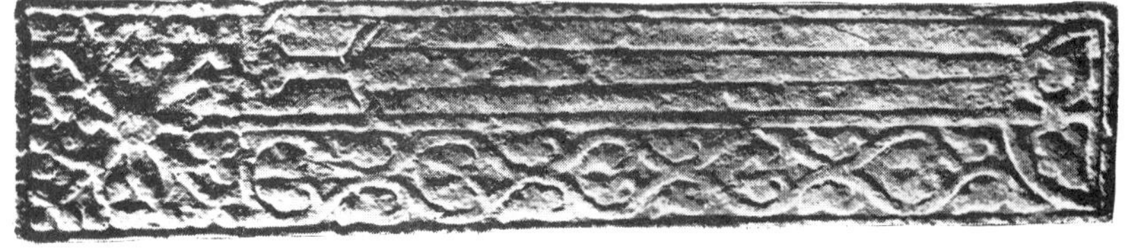
b

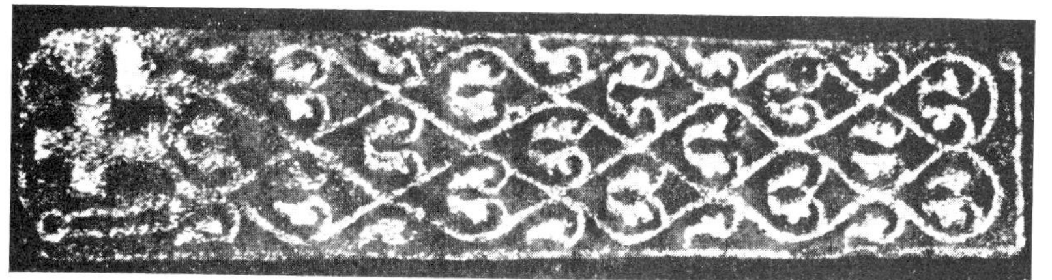

d

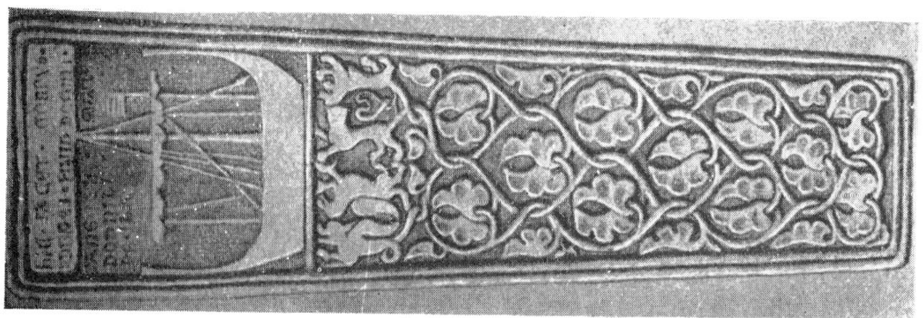

c

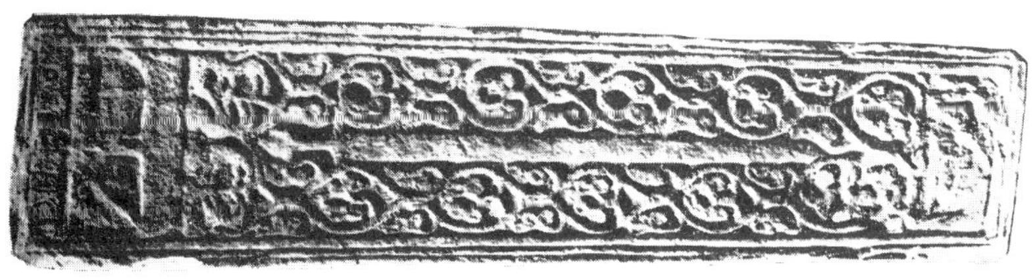

b

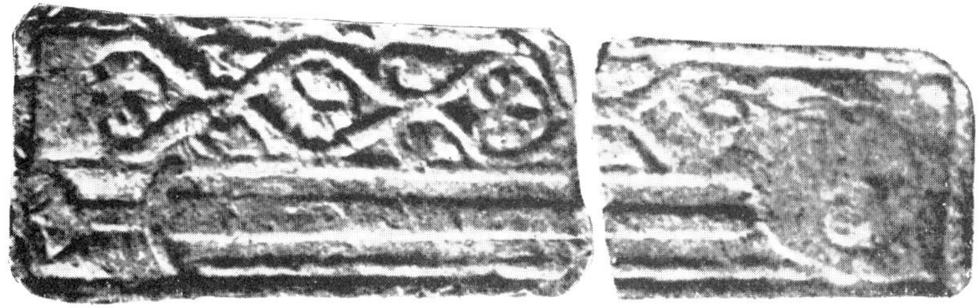

a

Plate XVI

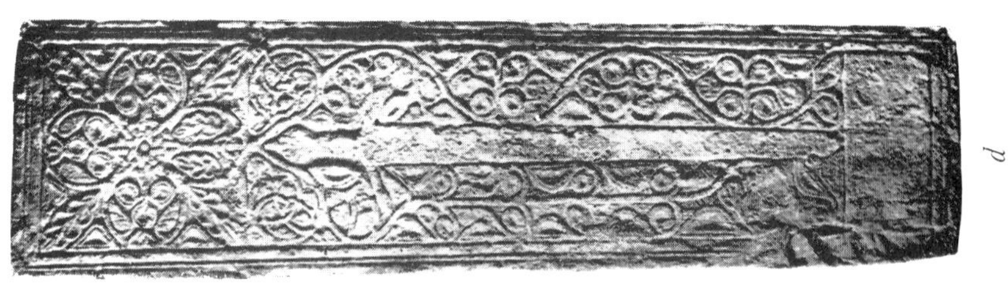

d

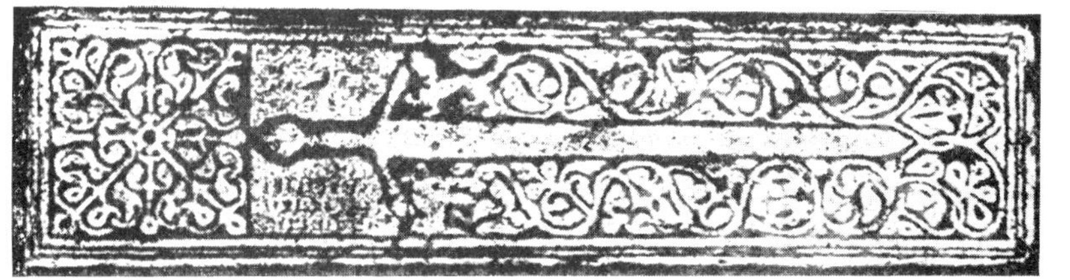

c

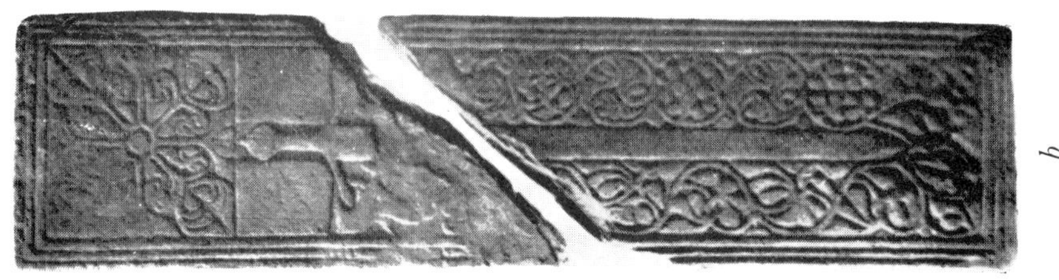

b

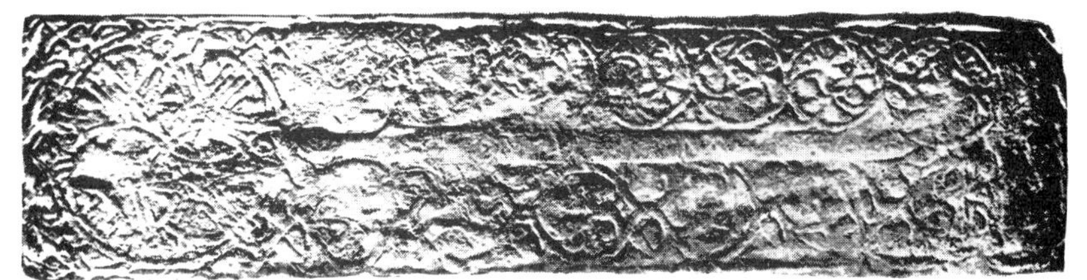

a

PLATE XVII

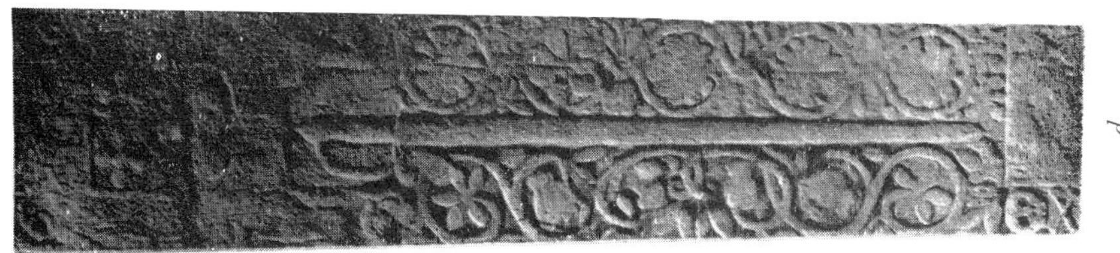

d

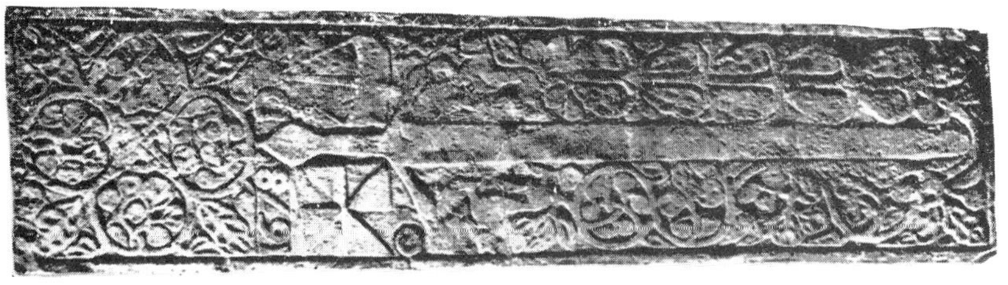

c

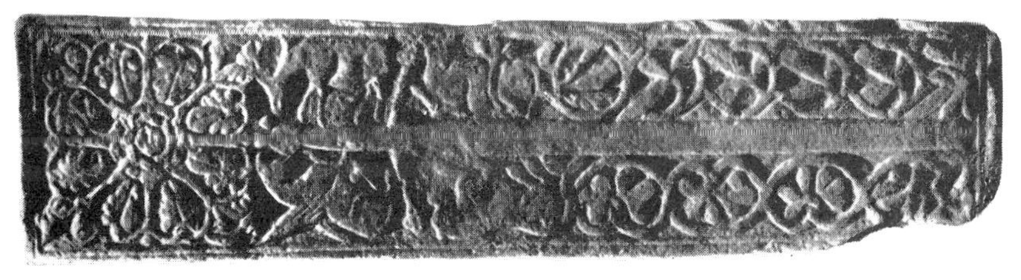

b

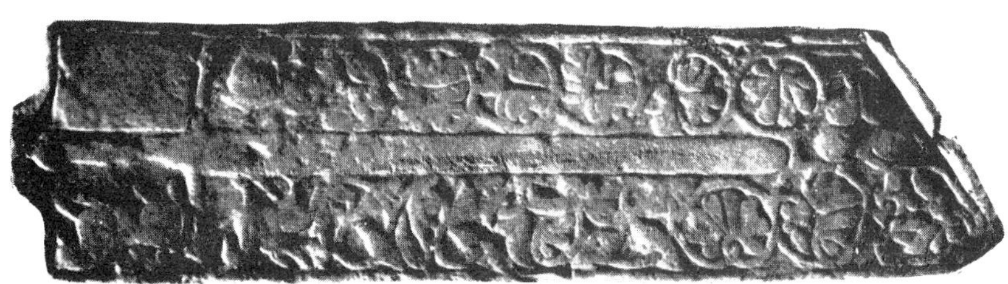

a

Plate XVIII

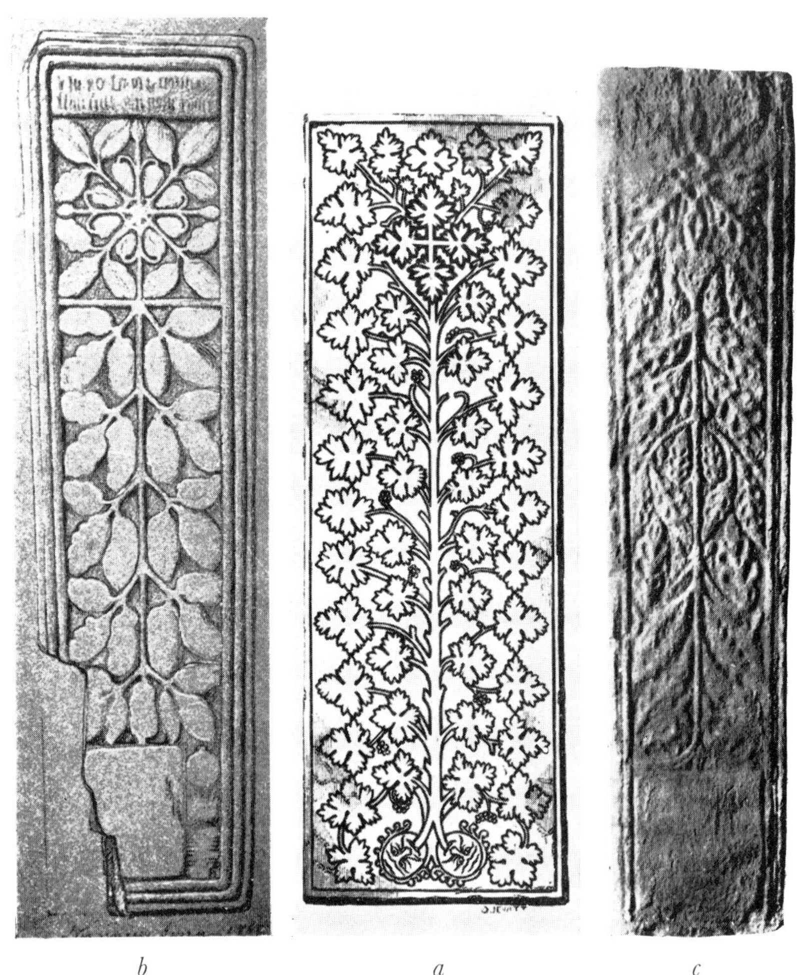

b *a* *c*

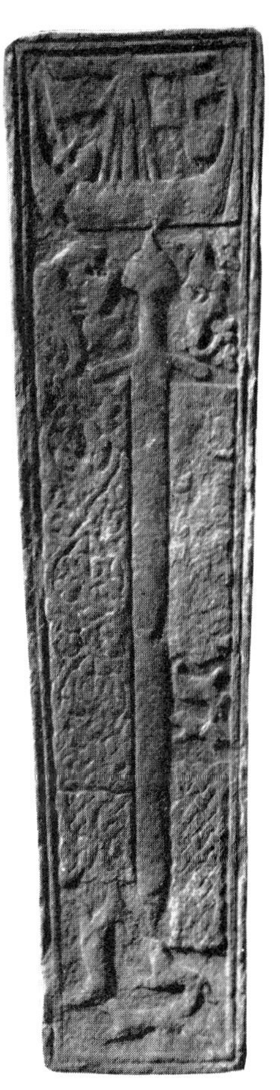

a

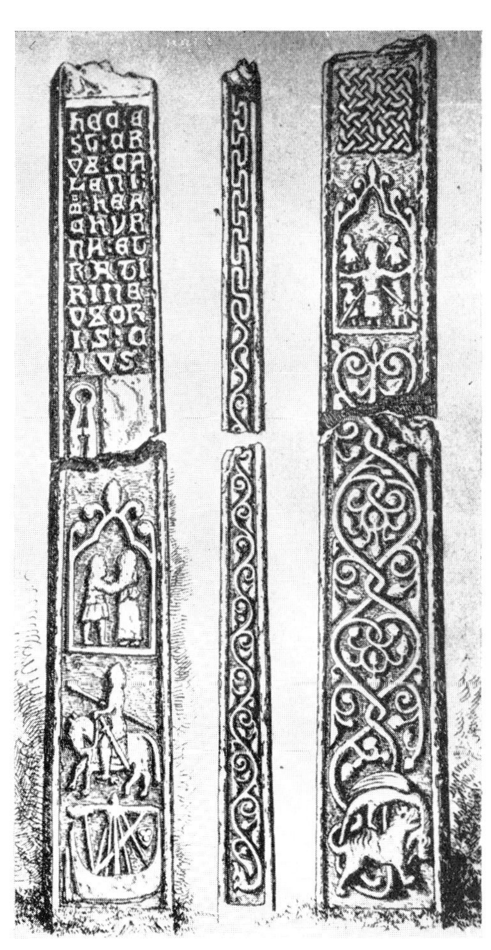

b

Plate XX

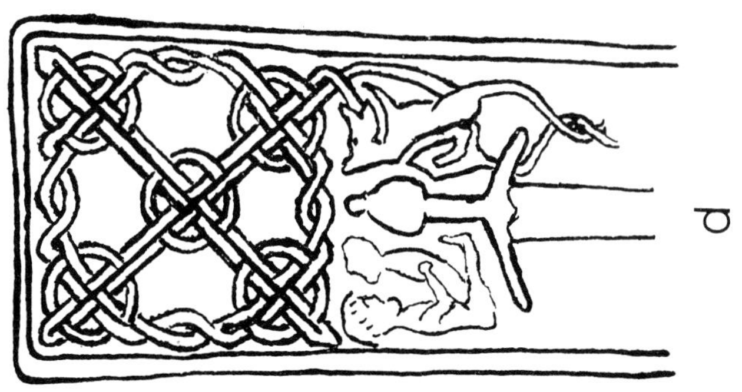

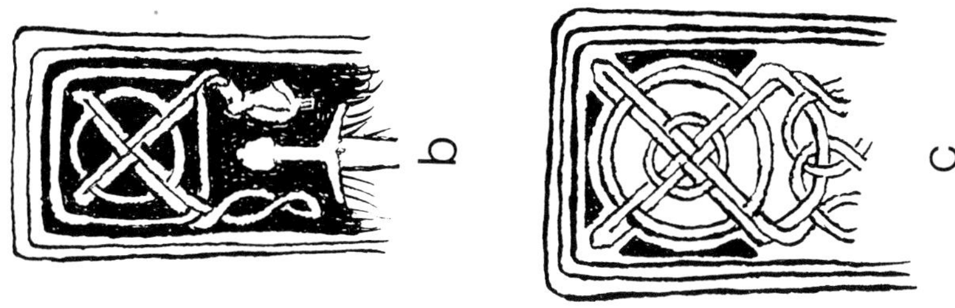

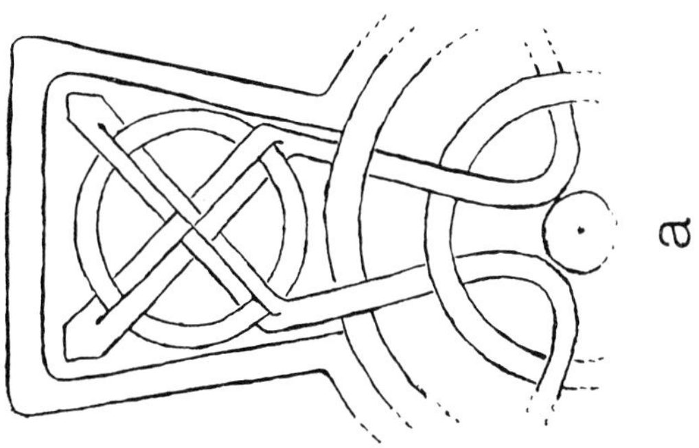

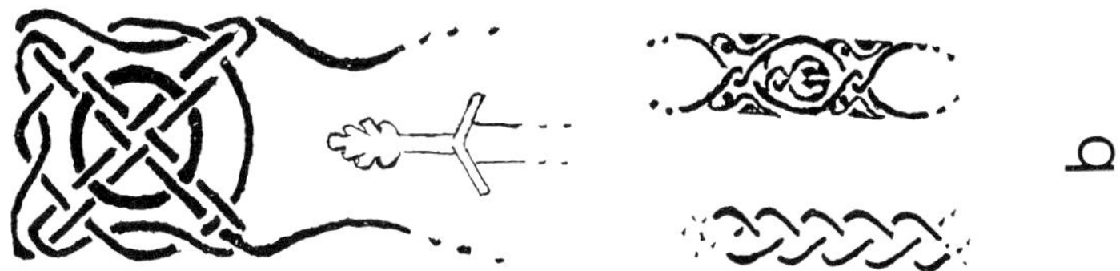

b

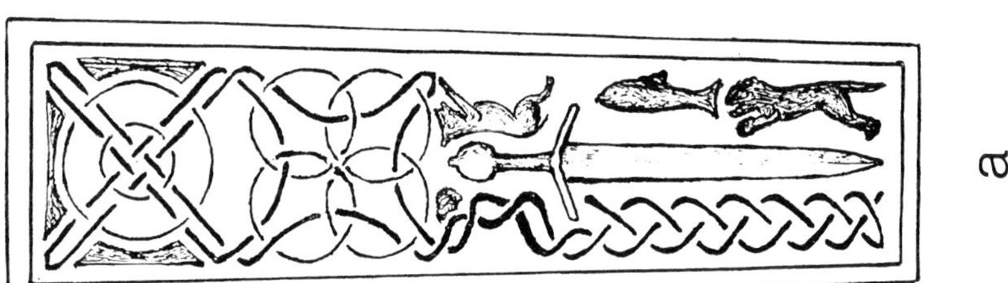

a

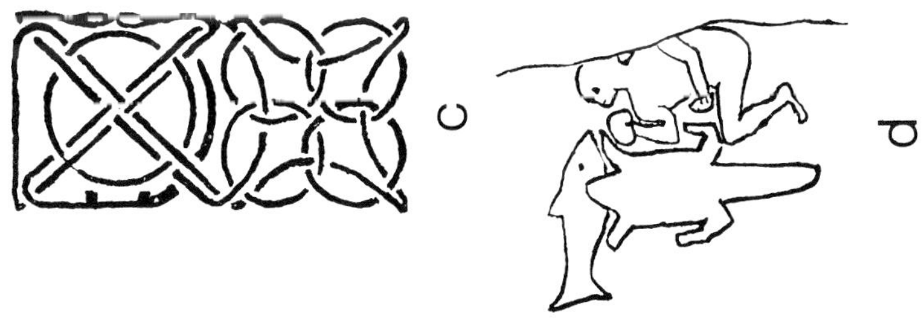

c

d

Plate XXII

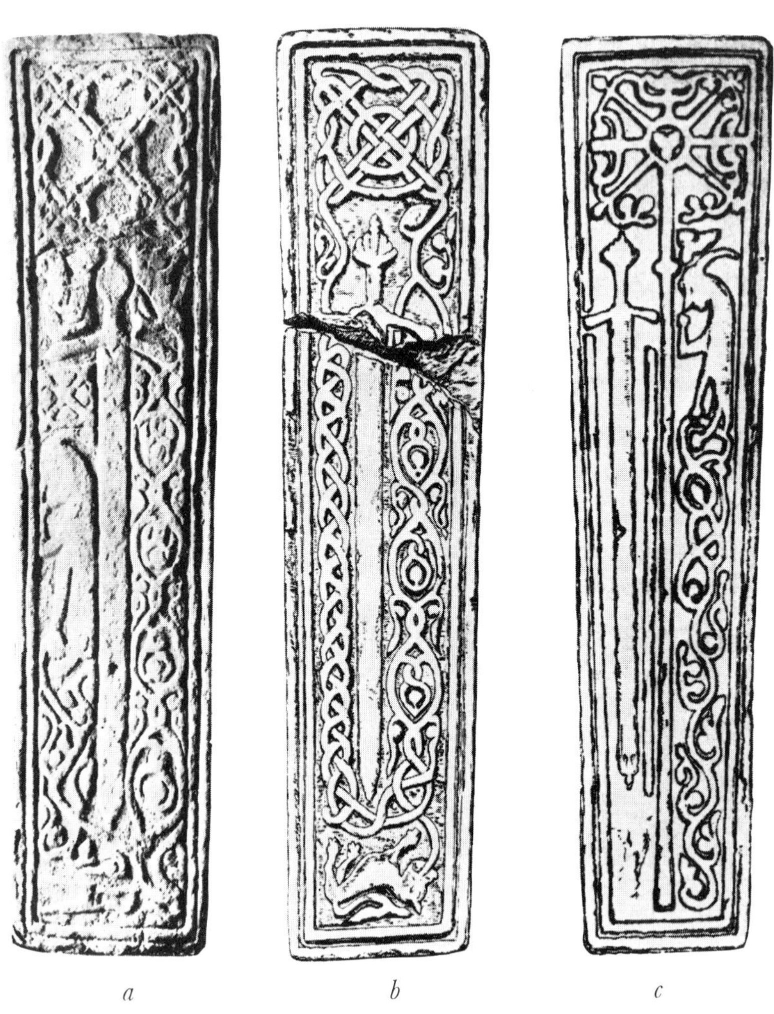

a *b* *c*

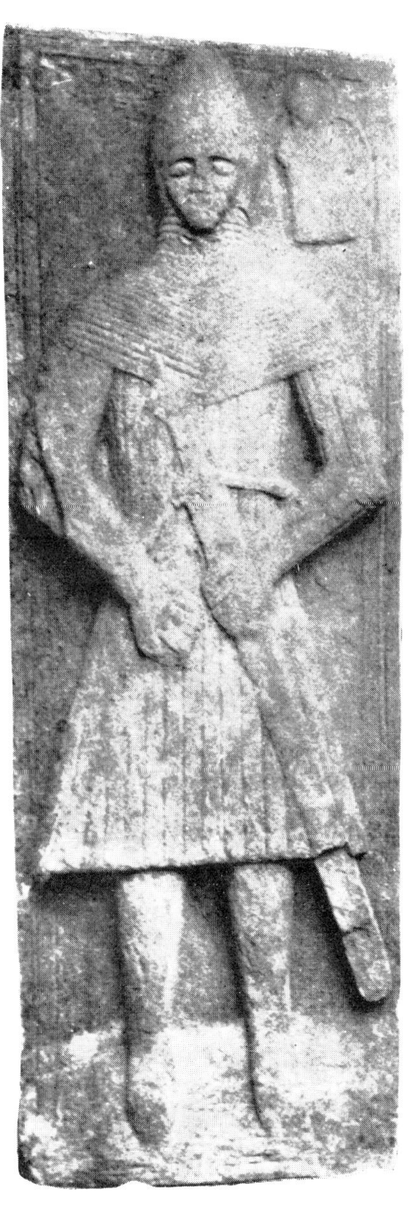

a

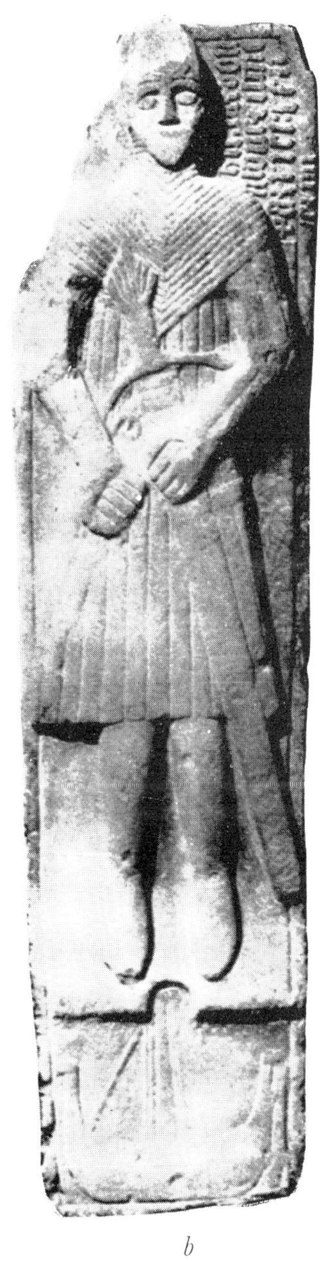

b

PLATE XXIV

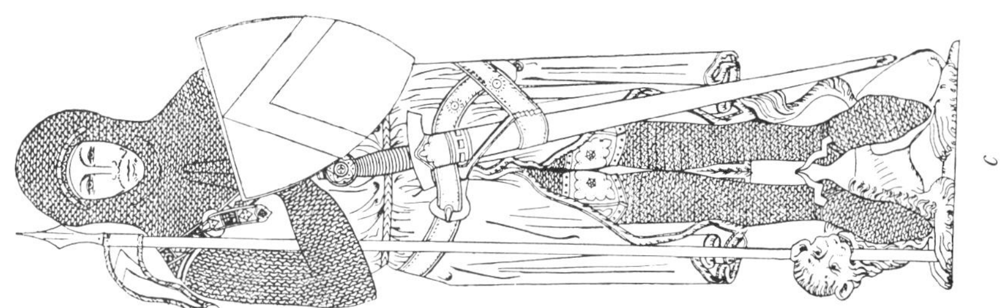

c

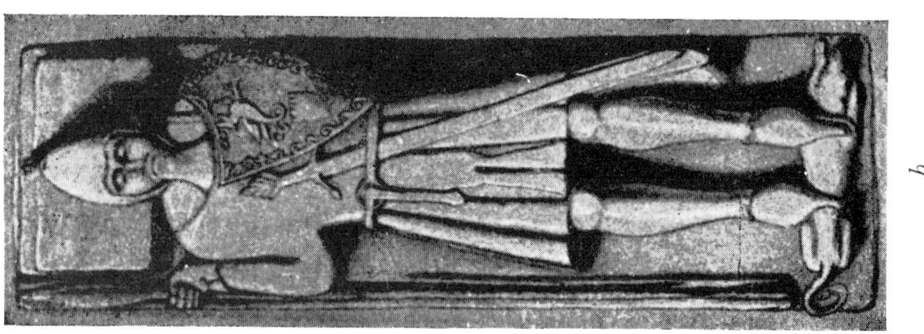

b

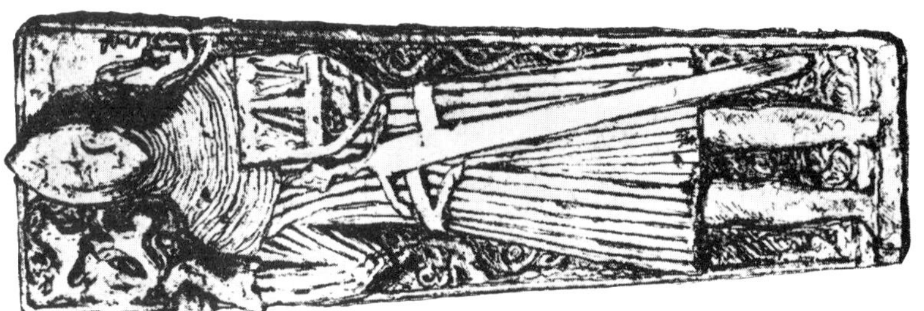

a

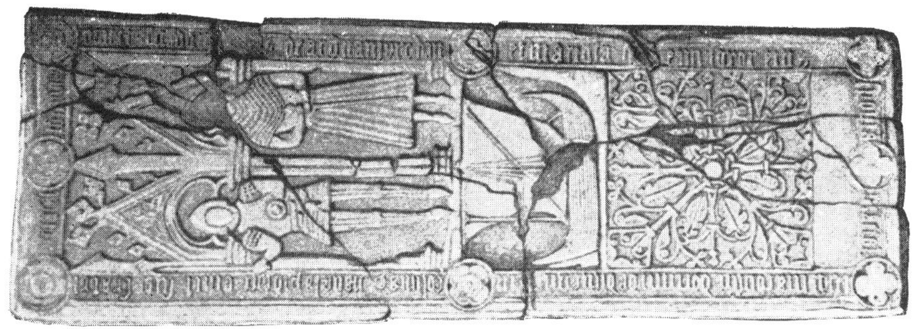

c

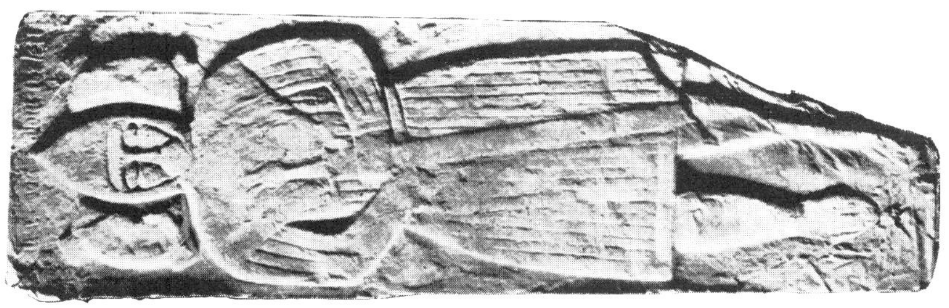

a

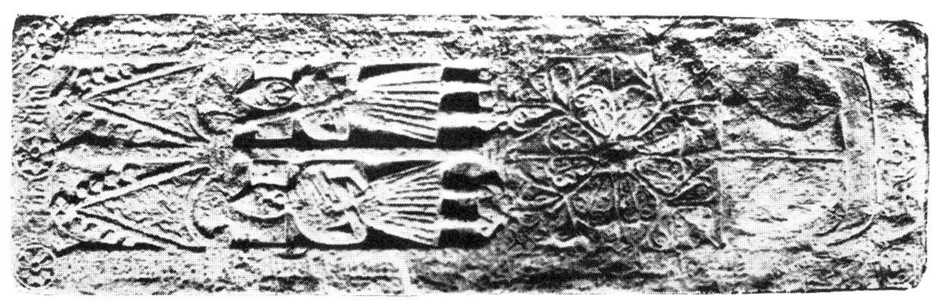

b

Plate XXVI

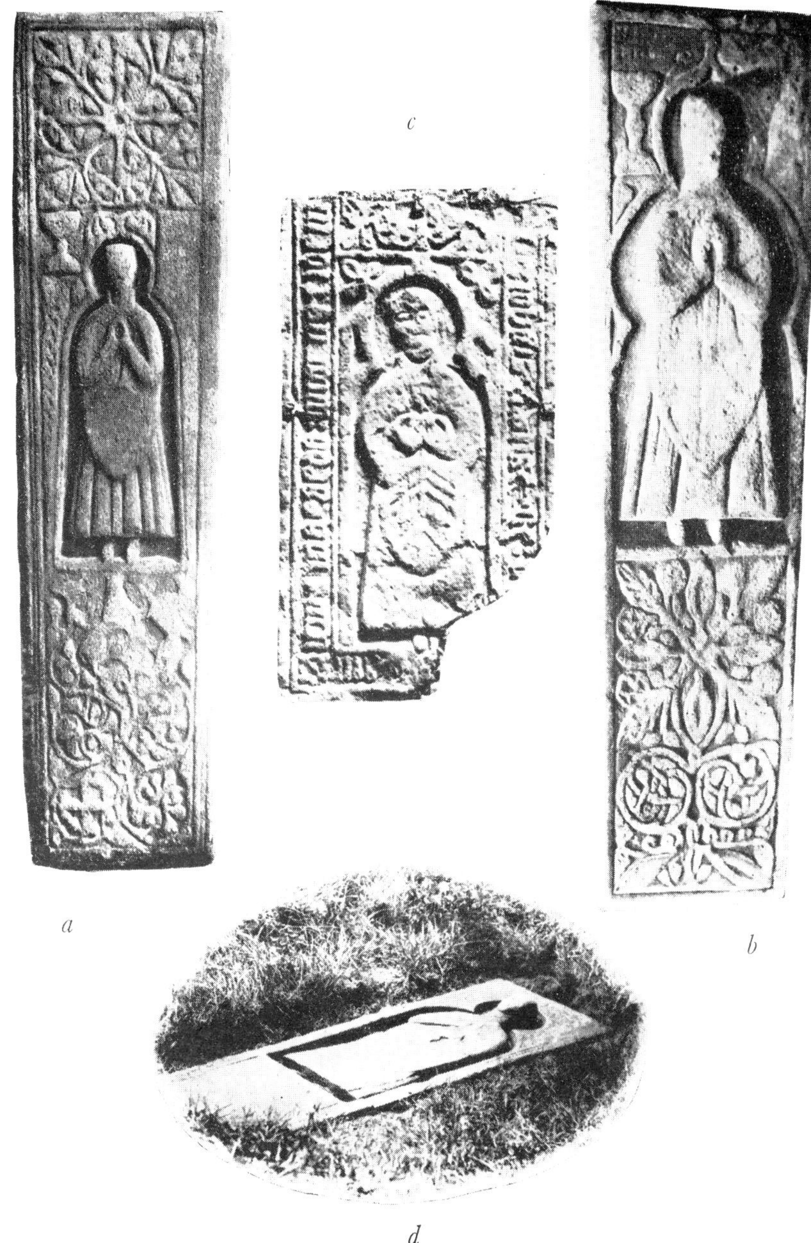

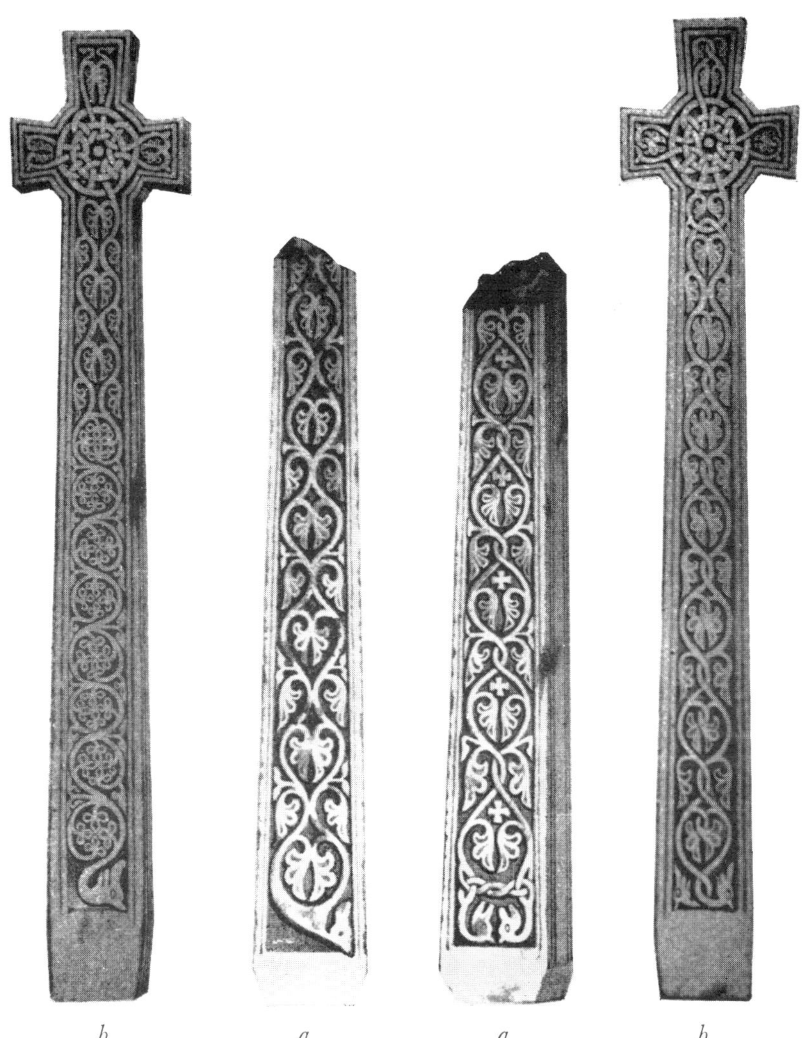

b *a* *a* *b*

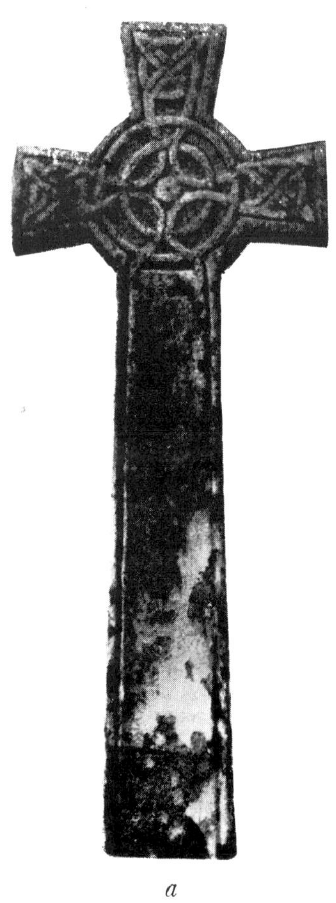

a

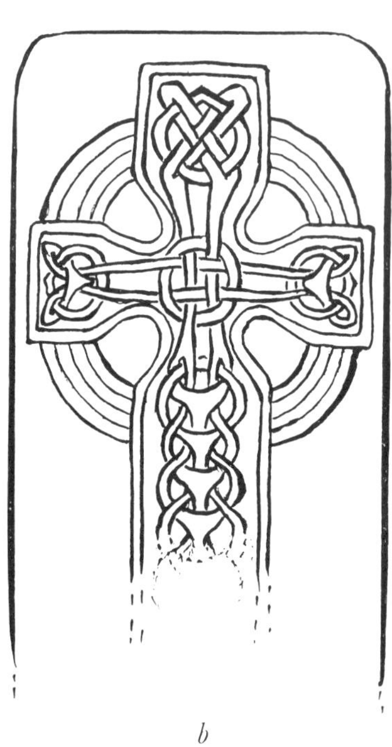

b

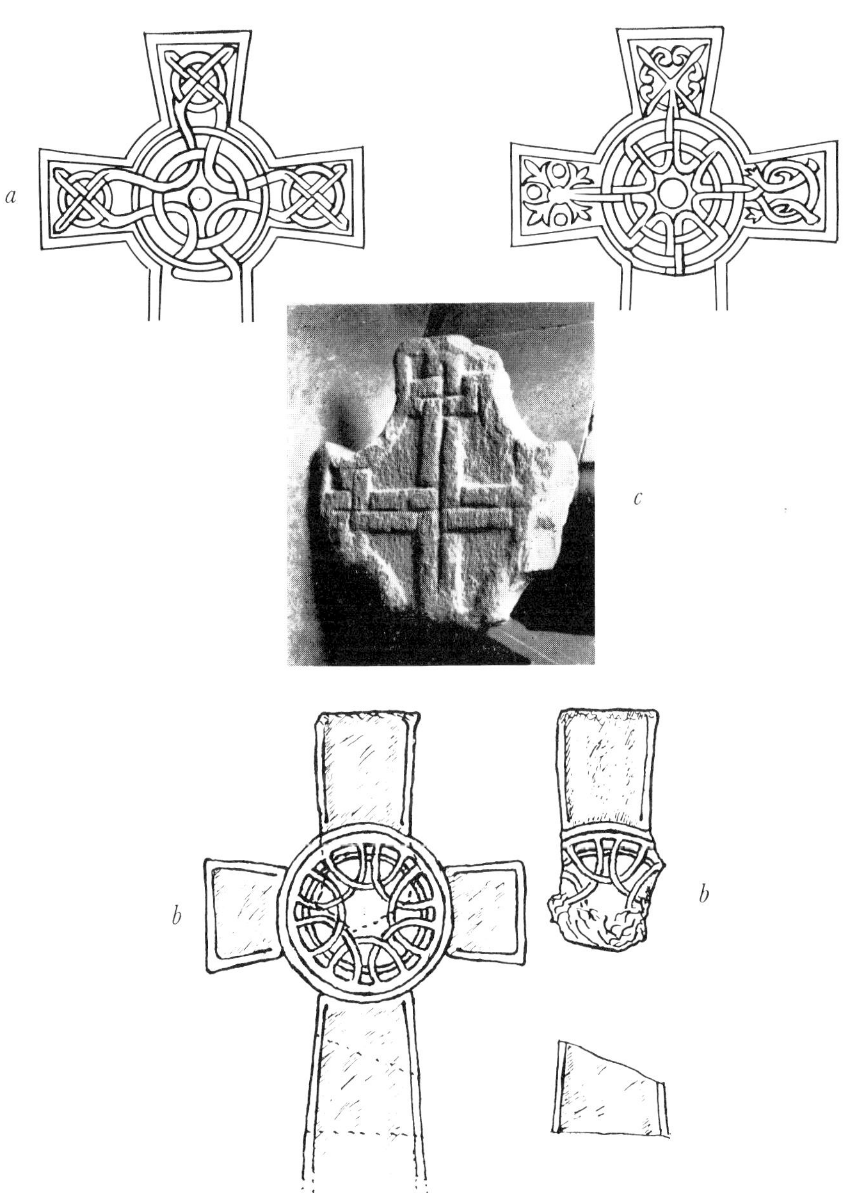
a
a
c
b
b

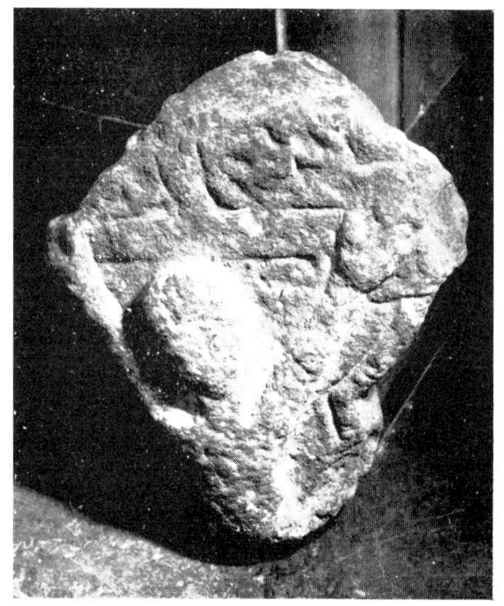

a

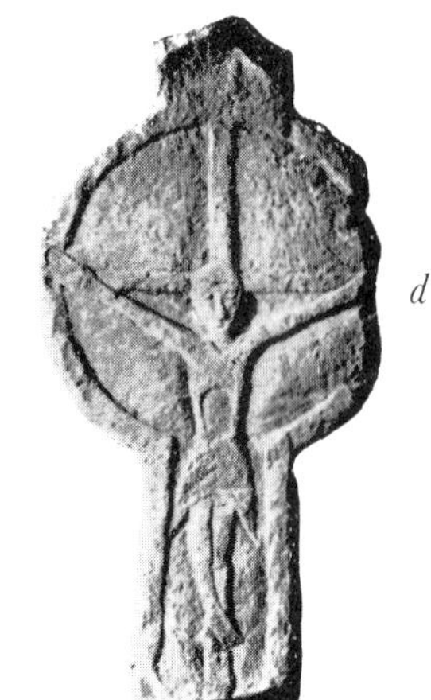

d

b

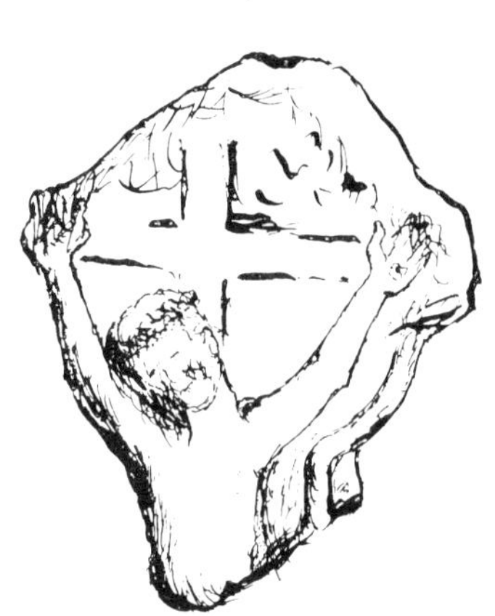

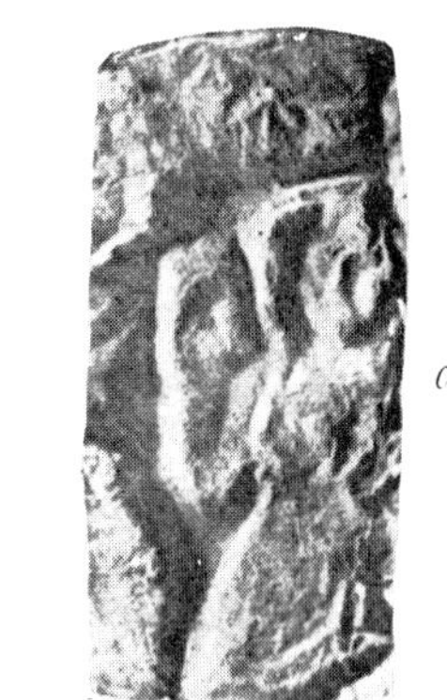

c

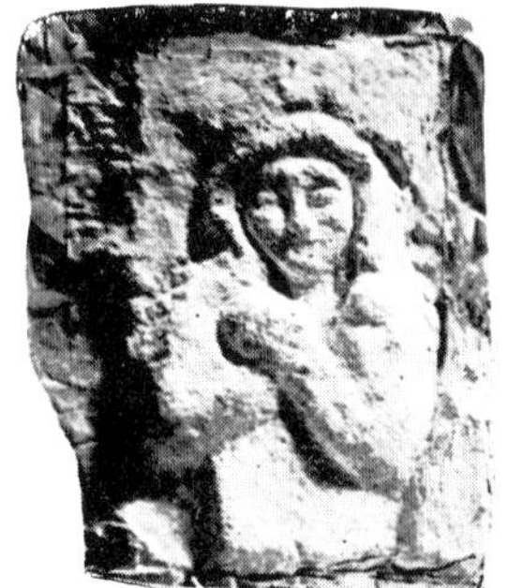

c

Plate XXXI

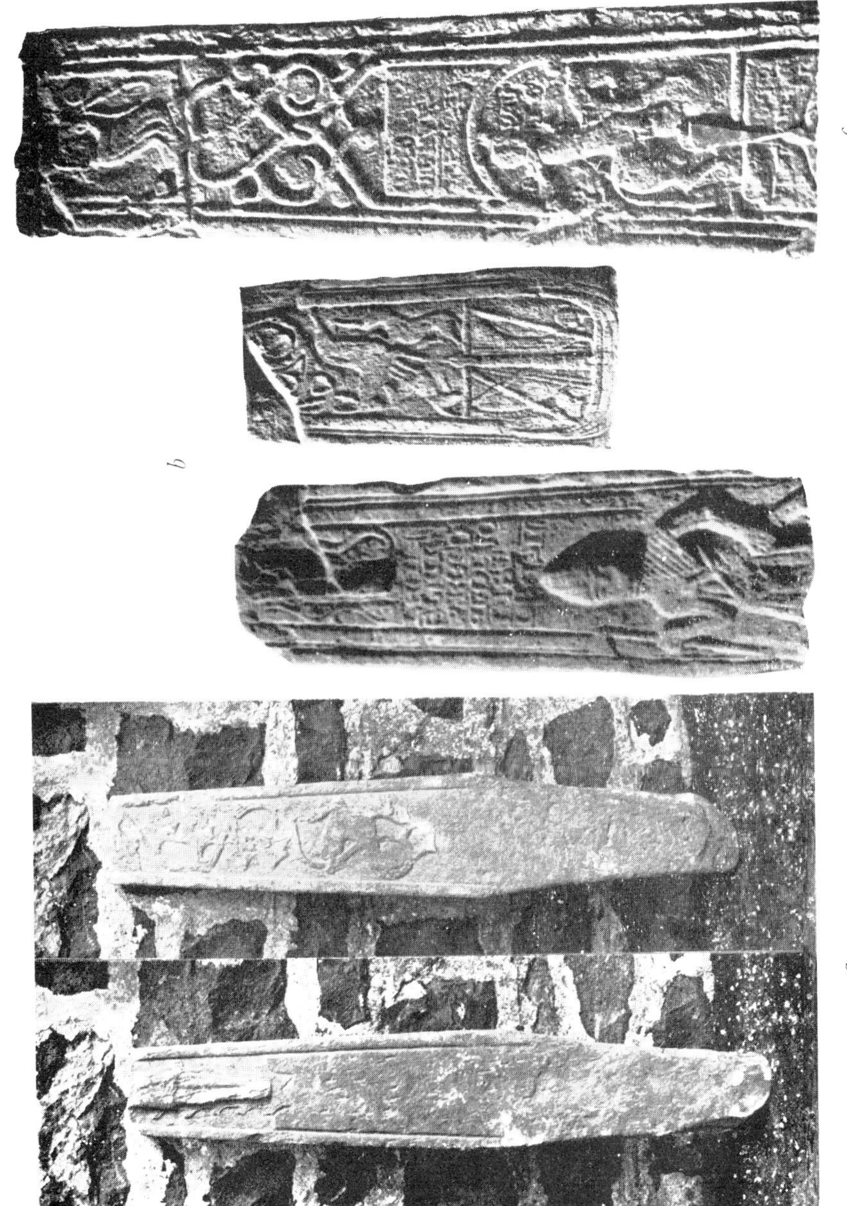

PLATE XXXII

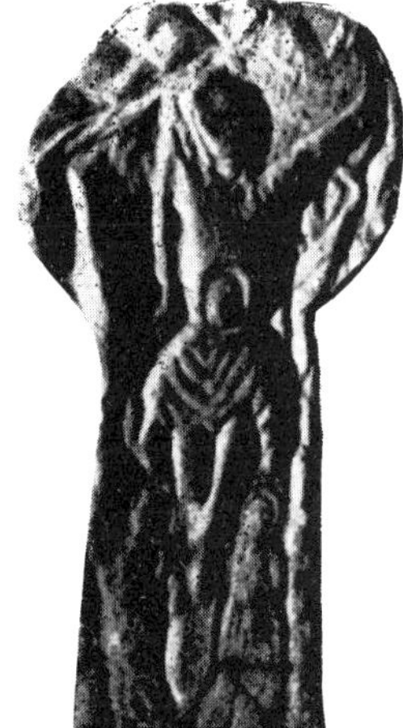

a

a

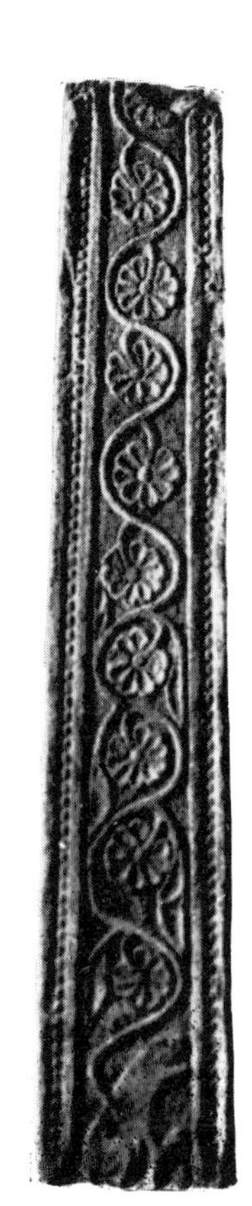

b

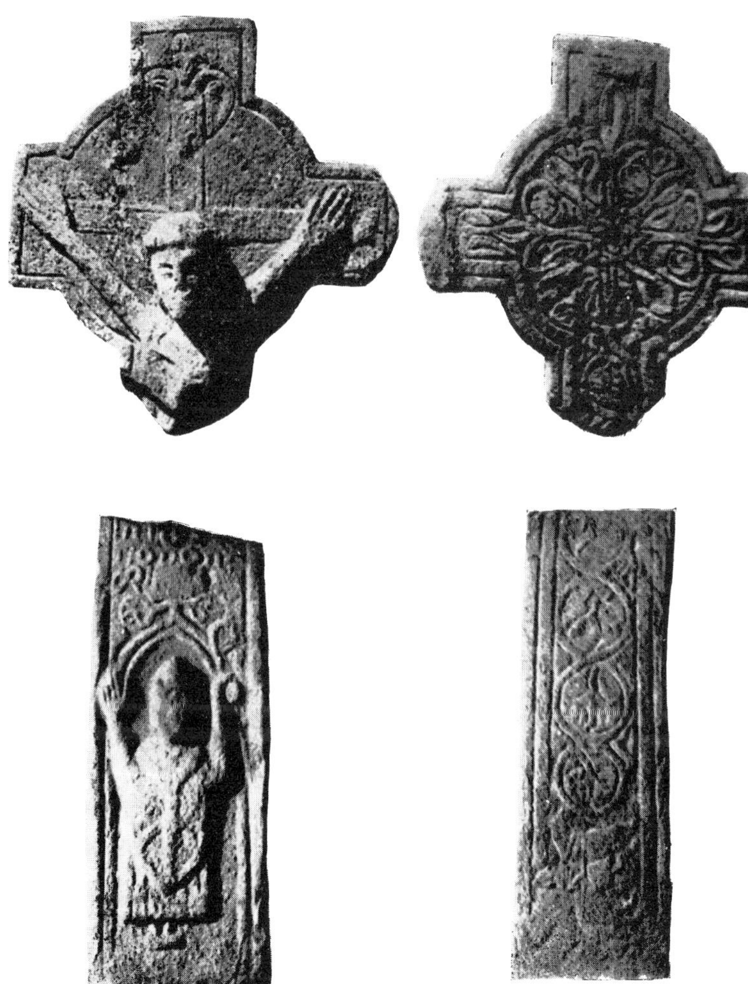

Plate XXXIV

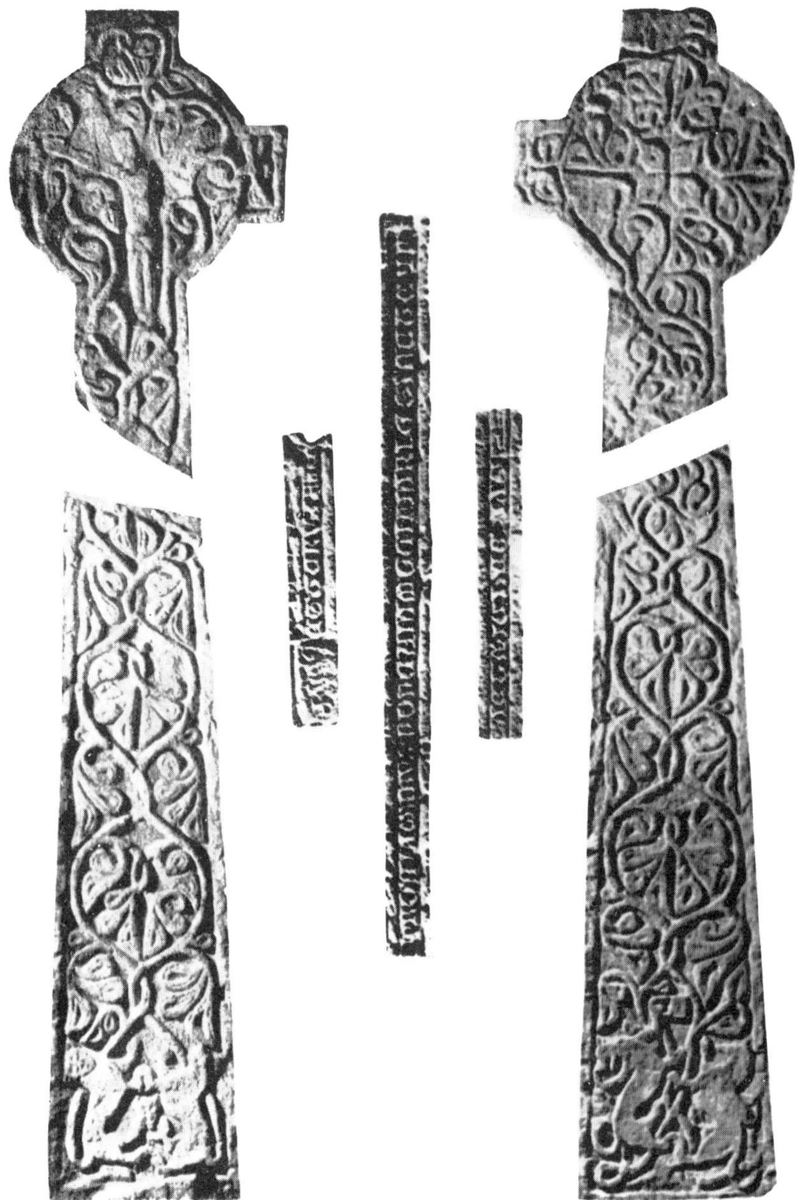

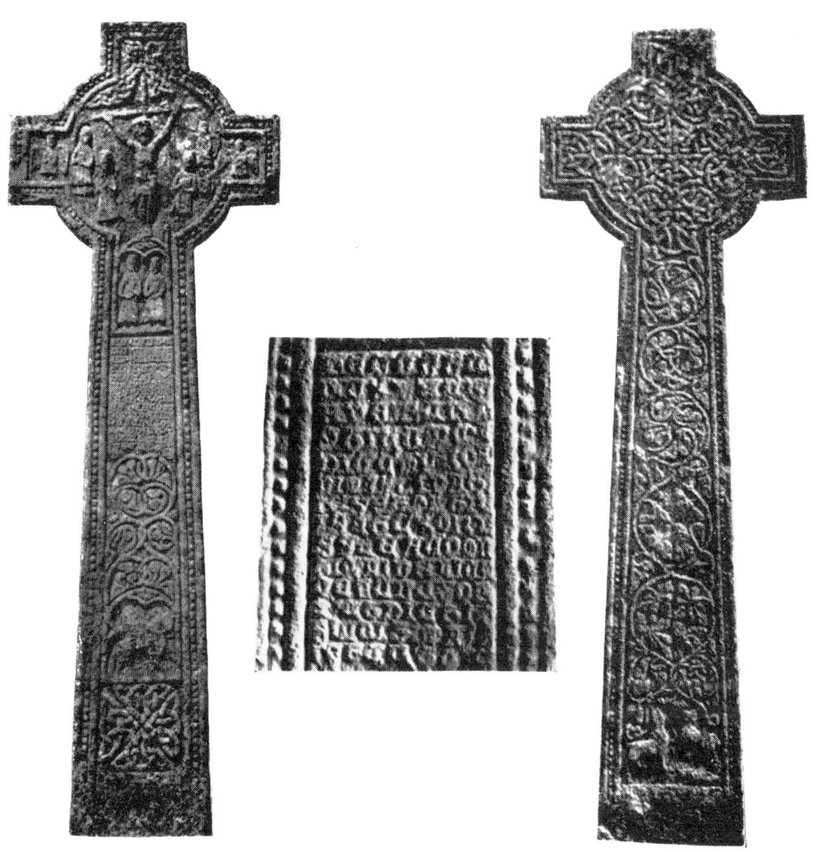